T0247235

PLAY ON SHAKESPEARE

Cymbeline

PLAY ON SHAKESPEARE

All's Well That Ends Well	Virginia Grise
Antony and Cleopatra	Christopher Chen
As You Like It	David Ivers
The Comedy of Errors	Christina Anderson
Coriolanus	Sean San José
Cymbeline	Andrea Thome
Edward III	Octavio Solis
Hamlet	Lisa Peterson
Henry IV	Yvette Nolan
Henry V	Lloyd Suh
Henry VI	Douglas P. Langworthy
Henry VIII	Caridad Svich
Julius Caesar	Shishir Kurup
King John	Brighde Mullins
King Lear	Marcus Gardley
Love's Labour's Lost	Josh Wilder
Macbeth	Migdalia Cruz
Measure for Measure	Aditi Brennan Kapil
The Merchant of Venice	Elise Thoron
The Merry Wives of Windsor	Dipika Guha
A Midsummer Night's Dream	Jeffrey Whitty
Much Ado About Nothing	Ranjit Bolt
Othello	Mfoniso Udofia
Pericles	Ellen McLaughlin
Richard II	Naomi Iizuka
Richard III	Migdalia Cruz
Romeo and Juliet	Hansol Jung
The Taming of the Shrew	Amy Freed
The Tempest	Kenneth Cavander
Timon of Athens	Kenneth Cavander
Titus Andronicus	Amy Freed
Troilus and Cressida	Lillian Groag
Twelfth Night	Alison Carey
The Two Gentlemen of Verona	Amelia Roper
The Two Noble Kinsmen	Tim Slover
The Winter's Tale	Tracy Young

Cymbeline

by
William Shakespeare

Modern verse translation by
Andrea Thome

Dramaturgy by
John Dias

Arizona State University
Tempe, Arizona
2024

Copyright ©2024 Andrea Thome.
All rights reserved. No part of this script may be reproduced in any form
or by any electronic or mechanical means including information storage
or retrieval systems without the written permission of the author. All
performance rights reside with the author. For performance permission,
contact: Play On Shakespeare, PO Box 955, Ashland, OR 97520,
info@playonshakespeare.org

*Publication of Play On Shakespeare is assisted by
generous support from the Hitz Foundation.
For more information, please visit* www.playonshakespeare.org

———

Published by ACMRS Press
Arizona Center for Medieval and Renaissance Studies,
Arizona State University, Tempe, Arizona
www.acmrspress.com

Library of Congress Cataloging-in-Publication Data
Names: Thome, Andrea, author. | Dias, John, contributor. | Shakespeare,
    William, 1564-1616. Cymbeline.
Title: Cymbeline / by Williams Shakespeare ; modern verse translation by
    Andrea Thome ; dramaturgy by John Dias.
Description: Tempe, Arizona : ACMRS Press, 2023. | Series: Play on
    Shakespeare | Summary: "The British king and his daughter star in
    a tale of deceit, jealousy, and accusations of infidelity, in updated
    language for modern audiences"-- Provided by publisher.
Identifiers: LCCN 2023044991 (print) | LCCN 2023044992 (ebook) |
    ISBN 9780866987912 (paperback) | ISBN 9780866987929 (ebook)
Subjects: LCSH: Britons--Kings and rulers--Drama. | Great Britain-
    -History--Roman period, 55 B.C.-449 A.D.--Drama. | Fathers and
    daughters--Drama. | Stepmothers--Drama. | Married people--Drama.
    | LCGFT: Historical drama. | Romantic plays. | Tragicomedies. |
    Adaptations.
Classification: LCC PR2878.C7 T46 2023 (print) | LCC PR2878.C7
    (ebook) | DDC 812/.6--dc23/eng/20230926
LC record available at https://lccn.loc.gov/2023044991
LC ebook record available at https://lccn.loc.gov/2023044992

Printed in the United States of America

We wish to acknowledge our gratitude
for the extraordinary generosity of the
Hitz Foundation

∽

Special thanks to the Play on Shakespeare staff
Lue Douthit, President and Co-Founder
Taylor Bailey, Producing Director
Cheryl Rizzo, Business Director
Artie Calvert, Finance Director

∽

Originally commissioned by the
Oregon Shakespeare Festival
Bill Rauch, Artistic Director
Cynthia Rider, Executive Director

SERIES PREFACE
PLAY ON SHAKESPEARE

In 2015, the Oregon Shakespeare Festival announced a new commissioning program. It was called "Play on!: 36 playwrights translate Shakespeare." It elicited a flurry of reactions. For some people this went too far: "You can't touch the language!" For others, it didn't go far enough: "Why not new adaptations?" I figured we would be on the right path if we hit the sweet spot in the middle.

Some of the reaction was due not only to the scale of the project, but its suddenness: 36 playwrights, along with 38 dramaturgs, had been commissioned and assigned to translate 39 plays, and they were already hard at work on the assignment. It also came fully funded by the Hitz Foundation with the shocking sticker price of $3.7 million.

I think most of the negative reaction, however, had to do with the use of the word "translate." It's been difficult to define precisely. It turns out that there is no word for the kind of subtle and rigorous examination of language that we are asking for. We don't mean "word for word," which is what most people think of when they hear the word translate. We don't mean "paraphrase," either.

The project didn't begin with 39 commissions. Linguist John McWhorter's musings about translating Shakespeare is what sparked this project. First published in his 1998 book *Word on the Street* and reprinted in 2010 in *American Theatre* magazine, he notes that the "irony today is that the Russians, the French, and other people in foreign countries possess Shakespeare to a much greater extent than we do, for the simple reason that they get to enjoy Shakespeare in the language they speak."

This intrigued Dave Hitz, a long-time patron of the Oregon Shakespeare Festival, and he offered to support a project that looked at Shakespeare's plays through the lens of the English we speak today. How much has the English language changed since Shakespeare? Is it possible that there are conventions in the early modern English of Shakespeare that don't translate to us today, especially in the moment of hearing it spoken out loud as one does in the theater?

How might we "carry forward" the successful communication between actor and audience that took place 400 years ago? "Carry forward," by the way, is what we mean by "translate." It is the fourth definition of *translate* in the Oxford English Dictionary.

As director of literary development and dramaturgy at the Oregon Shakespeare Festival, I was given the daunting task of figuring out how to administer the project. I began with Kenneth Cavander, who translates ancient Greek tragedies into English. I figured that someone who does that kind of work would lend an air of seriousness to the project. I asked him how might he go about translating from the source language of early modern English into the target language of contemporary modern English?

He looked at different kinds of speech: rhetorical and poetical, soliloquies and crowd scenes, and the puns in comedies. What emerged from his tinkering became a template for the translation commission. These weren't rules exactly, but instructions that every writer was given.

First, do no harm. There is plenty of the language that doesn't need translating. And there is some that does. Every playwright had different criteria for assessing what to change.

Second, go line-by-line. No editing, no cutting, no "fixing." I want the whole play translated. We often cut the gnarly bits in

Shakespeare for performance. What might we make of those bits if we understood them in the moment of hearing them? Might we be less compelled to cut?

Third, all other variables stay the same: the time period, the story, the characters, their motivations, and their thoughts. We designed the experiment to examine the language.

Fourth, and most important, the language must follow the same kind of rigor and pressure as the original, which means honoring the meter, rhyme, rhetoric, image, metaphor, character, action, and theme. Shakespeare's astonishingly compressed language must be respected. Trickiest of all: making sure to work within the structure of the iambic pentameter.

We also didn't know which of Shakespeare's plays might benefit from this kind of investigation: the early comedies, the late tragedies, the highly poetic plays. So we asked three translators who translate plays from other languages into English to examine a Shakespeare play from each genre outlined in the *First Folio*: Kenneth took on *Timon of Athens,* a tragedy; Douglas Langworthy worked on the *Henry the Sixth* history plays, and Ranjit Bolt tried his hand at the comedy *Much Ado about Nothing.*

Kenneth's *Timon* received a production at the Alabama Shakespeare in 2014 and it was on the plane ride home that I thought about expanding the project to include 39 plays. And I wanted to do them all at once. The idea was to capture a snapshot of contemporary modern English. I couldn't oversee that many commissions, and when Ken Hitz (Dave's brother and president of the Hitz Foundation) suggested that we add a dramaturg to each play, the plan suddenly unfolded in front of me. The next day, I made a simple, but extensive, proposal to Dave on how to commission and develop 39 translations in three years. He responded immediately with "Yes."

My initial thought was to only commission translators who translate plays. But I realized that "carry forward" has other meanings. There was a playwright in the middle of the conversation 400 years ago. What would it mean to carry *that* forward?

For one thing, it would mean that we wanted to examine the texts through the lens of performance. I am interested in learning how a dramatist makes sense of the play. Basically, we asked the writers to create performable companion pieces.

I wanted to tease out what we mean by contemporary modern English, and so we created a matrix of writers who embodied many different lived experiences: age, ethnicity, gender-identity, experience with translations, geography, English as a second language, knowledge of Shakespeare, etc.

What the playwrights had in common was a deep love of language and a curiosity about the assignment. Not everyone was on board with the idea and I was eager to see how the experiment would be for them. They also pledged to finish the commission within three years.

To celebrate the completion of the translations, we produced a festival in June 2019 in partnership with The Classic Stage Company in New York to hear all 39 of them. Four hundred years ago I think we went to *hear* a play; today we often go to *see* a play. In the staged reading format of the Festival, we heard these plays as if for the first time. The blend of Shakespeare with another writer was seamless and jarring at the same time. Countless actors and audience members told us that the plays were understandable in ways they had never been before.

Now it's time to share the work. We were thrilled when Ayanna Thompson and her colleagues at the Arizona Center for Medieval and Renaissance Studies offered to publish the translations for us.

I ask that you think of these as marking a moment in time.

The editions published in this series are based on the scripts that were used in the Play on! Festival in 2019. For the purpose of the readings, there were cuts allowed and these scripts represent those reading drafts.

The original commission tasked the playwrights and dramaturg to translate the whole play. The requirement of the commission was for two drafts which is enough to put the ball in play. The real fun with these texts is when there are actors, a director, a dramaturg, and the playwright wrestling with them together in a rehearsal room.

The success of a project of this scale depends on the collaboration and contributions of many people. The playwrights and dramaturgs took the assignment seriously and earnestly and were humble and gracious throughout the development of the translations. Sally Cade Holmes and Holmes Productions, our producer since the beginning, provided a steady and calm influence.

We have worked with more than 1,200 artists in the development of these works. We have partnered with more than three dozen theaters and schools. Numerous readings and more than a dozen productions of these translations have been heard and seen in the United States as well as Canada, England, and the Czech Republic.

There is a saying in the theater that 80% of the director's job is taken care of when the production is cast well. Such was my luck when I hired Taylor Bailey, who has overseen every reading and workshop, and was the producer of the Festival in New York. Katie Kennedy has gathered all the essays, and we have been supported by the rest of the Play on Shakespeare team: Kamilah Long, Summer Martin, and Amrita Ramanan.

All of this has come to be because Bill Rauch, then artistic director of the Oregon Shakespeare Festival, said yes when Dave

Hitz pitched the idea to him in 2011. Actually he said, "Hmm, interesting," which I translated to "yes." I am dearly indebted to that 'yes.'

My gratitude to Dave, Ken, and the Hitz Foundation can never be fully expressed. Their generosity, patience, and unwavering belief in what we are doing has given us the confidence to follow the advice of Samuel Beckett: "Ever tried. Ever failed. No matter. Try again. Fail again. Fail better."

Play on!

Dr. Lue Douthit
CEO/Creative Director at Play on Shakespeare
October 2020

WHAT WAS I THINKING?

Cymbeline
by Andrea Thome

Edited transcript from a *Cymbeline* post-show talkback of a Zoom reading of *Cymbeline* at SUNY New Paltz, Fall 2020.

I took on the crazy, wild, messy, beast of *Cymbeline* because I love this play — and its mess. I love its wild ride, its unhinged, unapologetic sense of play, and overflows of human feeling and imaginative vitality. People complain that *Cymbeline* is all over the place, but I relish how UN-neat it is in language and form, like its characters' hearts, leaking and exploding and healing again. What else is life? It splits itself open, exposes all our essential (and embarrassing) parts and needs, and doing so, finds wholeness.

When Lue first called me up to explain the Play On! project, we had never met; she had only read my play *Pinkolandia*. She explained her wild proposal — "I'm super interested!" I told her — then she said, "Well here's the play I was thinking about for you ..." And in my head, I'm whispering "*Cymbeline*!" because it's a play that had always fascinated me, one I tried to unravel in a college design project ("How can this play possibly be staged?" I wondered), but I hadn't said anything out loud to Lue. So when she said, "*Cymbeline*," I almost shouted "Yes!"

This made me immediately trust Lue as a dramaturg. I love (and often write) plays that travel between worlds, and there's an imaginative, mystical aspect to this one. There are also deep bonds and complicated dynamics between parents and children, and, you know, the usual rich Shakespearean conversations about life and death and how we should treat people: like the individual, inter-related human souls that we are, not transactionally, not as objects to serve our pride or bankruptcy (whether monetary or moral). Those are just a few more things I really love about this deep and worldly play. Also: it doesn't take itself too seriously, despite the utter seriousness and truth of its observations about life.

As a kid I participated in a program called The Young Shake-speare Players in Madison, Wisconsin. A wonderfully kind and brilliant man named Richard DiPrima founded and ran it. *[Richard sadly passed away in 2022, but the organization continues to thrive under the leadership of his co-director and wife, Anne DiPrima.]* Kids in the program do full Shakespeare plays — and yeah, some-times the performances could last forever, but always felt fresh, full of wonder — and it took me on an incredible journey of diving into and learning to understand Shakespeare's language. Richard would make these cassette tapes — I was a kid a long time ago! — explain-ing every single line, so you understood what it was saying. I played Ariel in *The Tempest,* and Leontes in *A Winter's Tale*. I always felt that even as a fifteen-year-old, I could get inside of this language, and it was mine. But then I went off to college, and Shakespeare once again felt distant, and that was often reinforced by produc-tions I saw that made it feel especially far away.

So when Lue came to me with this project, I didn't hesitate to say, "Yes, I believe in this." Because I think it's really important that people feel that Shakespeare is theirs, that the plays touch them inside the way they did when I was a kid. I didn't feel like "just" a teenage Ariel, or that the eight-year-old who played the gravedig-ger in *Hamlet* was just a little kid, because even if initially we didn't understand every image (and how many adults do, honestly?), we understood and connected to those feelings in a real way. Rich-ard opened up the door into the language, but then respected and trusted us to find our own ways of connecting and identifying with the characters and stories. So, the trick with this Play On! assignment was to try to maintain the sublimeness of these images, and the verbal and imaginative games that Shakespeare is playing, while also helping open a new path into this complex, layered, emotional, and philosophical terrain. As a writer, figuring out how to do that is terrifying.

I translate a lot of theatrical work from Spanish to English, especially work from Mexico. (I helped start, and ran, the Lark Play Development Center's México-U.S. Playwright Exchange.) I used to be a dancer, and translating can be like when you're doing a new choreographer's work. You have to develop new ways of moving through space, and new ways of making your body contort and gesture in different ways — but it's still your body, and the movement still has to be expressed through your own arms and legs and spine. Once you've done work by a particular choreographer, you've developed new muscles, and those muscles are now part of you, and those ways of inhabiting space are part of you, and you take that all with you to the next dance. So, that's how I feel when I have to translate a playwright's world from Spanish to English, and I feel that same way about the assignment to "translate" *Cymbeline*, from Shakespeare's world to ours. You have to get inside it, and let it get inside of you. You have to try to understand how this choreographer/playwright is moving through their world, moving through language, how the thought processes are working, the little games that they're doing. And then you have to embody it, manifest it through your own sensibility to forms, sounds, air, time, and space, and through your own human heart.

It took me forever to do a first draft for this play because it's massive, but also, I would get lost in one paragraph or one little section of verse and would ask, "Oye Will, what are you doing here?" It felt like this living conversation. I chose John Dias as my dramaturg because I wanted a friend who knew my process really well (he had produced another new play of mine). And it didn't hurt that he has a deep knowledge about Shakespeare. He patiently went through each agonizing beat with me.

We had an early development workshop at the Illinois Shakespeare Festival in 2017, even though I only had translated half of the play. I wanted to hear what I was setting up, to learn how it lived in time and space. We had another workshop at The Lark, and just before the Festival in 2019, we had a quick workshop just so I could hear the fifth act. I mean it when I say that I worked slowly on this translation: whenever I came back to it, I would enter it again from the beginning of the draft, get re-acquainted with its waters, and work a little bit further each time.

Now that I'm on the other side of the process, I know that I've learned so much from Shakespeare as a playwright, and I've learned so much about my process — and this new understanding, these new visceral and mental expansions will be part of me through every play I write from now on. When people get really upset about the idea of Play On! and say, "Oh how dare you do that to Shakespeare!" I say, "This is a bringing together. This project brings Shakespeare so much closer to these thirty-six playwrights who now carry it in our bones and muscles."

I hope that you enjoy the read. There are still many spots that I don't think I got right, but as Lue said, "Let's share this now, so people know what you've been thinking about with this play. We're setting up a conversation."

— Andrea Thome

CHARACTERS IN THE PLAY

(in order of speaking)

FIRST GENTLEMAN

SECOND GENTLEMAN

QUEEN, Cymbeline's second wife and Cloten's mother

POSTHUMUS LEONATUS, Imogen's husband, adopted as an orphan and raised in Cymbeline's family

IMOGEN, Cymbeline's daughter by a former queen and Cloten's stepsister

CYMBELINE, the King and Imogen's father

PISANIO, Posthumus's servant

FIRST LORD

CLOTEN, the Queen's son by a former husband and Imogen's stepbrother

SECOND LORD

LADY, Imogen's lady

IACHIMO, a Roman lord and Philario's friend

PHILARIO, Posthumus's host in Rome

FRENCHMAN, a gentleman

CORNELIUS, court physician

CAIUS LUCIUS, Roman ambassador and later general

BELARIUS, banished lord living under the name Morgan, who abducted King Cymbeline's infant sons

GUIDERIUS, Cymbeline's son, kidnapped in childhood by Belarius and raised as his son, Polydore

ARVIRAGUS, Cymbeline's son, kidnapped in childhood by Belarius and raised as his son, Cadwal

FIRST SENATOR, a Roman senator

TRIBUNE

SECOND SENATOR, a Roman senator

CAPTAIN

SOOTHSAYER

FIRST CAPTAIN, a British captain

SECOND CAPTAIN, another British captain

FIRST JAILOR

SECOND JAILOR

SICILIUS LEONATUS, the ghost of Posthumus's father

MOTHER, the ghost of Posthumus's mother

FIRST BROTHER, the ghost of Posthumus's brother

SECOND BROTHER, the ghost of Posthumus's brother

JUPITER, King of the Gods in Roman Mythology

Other Lords, a **Dutchman,** a **Spaniard, Musicians, Messengers, Attendants, Roman Soldiers, British Soldiers, Prisoners, Officers,** and **Ladies**

ACT 1 ♦ SCENE 1

BRITAIN. CYMBELINE'S PALACE.

Two Gentlemen enter

FIRST GENTLEMAN

There's not a man who doesn't frown: the King's
Courtiers ape his moods more faithfully
Than our fates obey the stars.

SECOND GENTLEMAN

What's happened now?

FIRST GENT.

His daughter, heir to his kingdom (and intended   5
For the only son of his wife — a widow that
He recently had married) has given herself
To a poor but worthy gentleman. She's wedded,
Her husband banished; she imprisoned, while
The courtiers playact sorrow, though the King   10
Is truly afflicted.

SECOND GENT.

Only the King?

FIRST GENT.

Lord Cloten, who lost her, too: so is the Queen,
Who so desired the match. But not one courtier,
Although they mask their faces so they match   15
The King's own looks, would deny they're glad
For just the thing that makes him scowl.

SECOND GENT.

Why is that?

FIRST GENT.

The one who's lost the Princess is a thing

1

Much worse than words portray; the one who won her   20
(I mean, that married her, poor decent soul,
And then was banished) is so extraordinary
That if you searched each corner of the earth
For one like him, you would find something lacking
In all whom you'd compare.   25

SECOND GENT.

But what's his name and birth?

FIRST GENT.

His roots I can't dig up: I know his father,
Sicilius, served well fighting 'gainst the Romans;
That's where he gained the surname Leonatus
And had two other sons, who died in war.   30
Their father, old, enamored of his sons,
From sorrow quit this life; and then his lady,
Carrying this gentleman (our theme) died too,
As he was born. The King takes the babe under
His own protection, calls him Posthumus Leonatus,   35
Offers him all the learning one his age
Is able to absorb; this he breathed in
Like we take air, as fast as it was offered,
And blossoming, gave fruit: he lived in court
(Which as you know, is rare) most praised, most loved,   40
By young and old alike. As for his lady,
(For whom he's banished) the price that she has paid
Proves his great value to her; you cannot doubt
What kind of man he is.

SECOND GENT.

I honor him,   45
Just hearing how you praise him. But tell me please,
Is she the King's sole child?

FIRST GENT.

His only girl.

He had two sons (if this is worth your hearing,

Prick up your ears) the oldest one just three,   50

The baby in swaddling clothes when they were stolen

From their nursery; and still no one knows

Where they ended up.

SECOND GENT.

How long ago was this?

FIRST GENT.

Some twenty years.   55

SECOND GENT.

How can a king's children be taken just like that?

So laxly guarded, and so slow the search

That couldn't trace them!

FIRST GENT.

It's strange in every way,

So negligent it's almost laughable,   60

Yet it is true, sir.

SECOND GENT.

I believe you, truly.

FIRST GENT.

We should hush now. Here come the gentleman,

The Queen, and Princess.

They exit

ACT 1 ◆ SCENE 2

THE SAME PLACE

The Queen, Posthumus, and Imogen enter

QUEEN

No, be assured, daughter, you'll find that I

Prove wrong the unjust image of stepmothers

3

Treating you cruelly. You're my prisoner, but
Your jailor will provide you with the keys
That keep you locked at home. For you, Posthumus,   5
As soon as I win over the offended King,
I'll be your greatest advocate.

POSTHUMUS

With your leave,
I'll ride away today.

QUEEN

You know the peril.   10
I'll take a walk around the garden, and bemoan
The aching of forbidden love, even though
The King's decreed that you not speak together.

She exits

IMOGEN

Oh
Counterfeit courtesy! How well this tyrant   15
Can tickle where she wounds! My dearest husband,
I'm wary of my father's wrath, but not
Afraid (besides my daughterly respect)
Of what his rage can do. You must be gone,
And I will stay and bear the constant stabs   20
From angry eyes: my wretched life's sole comfort
Is that there is this jewel in the world,
That I might see again.

POSTHUMUS

My queen, my mistress:
Oh lady, weep no more, or I'll give cause   25
To be suspected of more tenderness
Than a man's dignity allows. I will remain
The loyalest husband that ever made vows.
I'll dwell for now in Rome with one Philario

Who to my father was a friend, to me   30
Known just through letters: write to me, my queen,
And with my eyes I'll drink the words you send,
Though the ink be made of bitterness.

The Queen re-enters

QUEEN

Be brief:
If the King comes, who knows how much I'll suffer   35
Of his displeasure: (*aside*) And yet I'll lure him
To walk this way: each time I do him wrong
He blindly buys the stings I sell as sweets,
Pays dear for my deceits.

She exits

POSTHUMUS

If our parting took   40
As long a time as we have left to live,
The agony of leaving would just grow. Goodbye!

IMOGEN

No, wait a little:
Even if you were riding out for air
This farewell would be too paltry. Look here, love;   45
This diamond was my mother's; take it, heart;
And keep it 'til you woo another wife,
When Imogen is dead.

POSTHUMUS

What's that? Another?
You gentle gods, give me just what I have,   50
And hold back my embraces of any other
With bonds of death! Remain, remain right here,

(*putting on the ring*)

'Til my senses feel no more: and sweetest, fairest,
Just as when I exchanged myself for you

5

You lost more in the bargain; now trading tokens   55
I'm dealt the better hand. Wear this for me,
It is a manacle of love. I'll place it
Upon this lovely prisoner.

Putting a bracelet on her arm

IMOGEN

Oh gods!
When will we meet again?   60

Enter Cymbeline and Lords

POSTHUMUS

Careful, the King!

CYMBELINE

You worm, lewd thing, get out, out of my sight!
If after this command you plague this court
With your unworthiness, you die. Away!
You're poison to my blood.   65

POSTHUMUS

The gods protect you,
And any loyal friends who remain in court.
I am gone.

He exits

IMOGEN

There cannot be a sting in death
More sharp than this.   70

CYMBELINE

Oh you disloyal thing,
You should be making me feel young and light,
Not weighing me down with cares that age me.

IMOGEN

Please,
Don't let your enraged fury make you ill;   75
My senses are numb to your wrath; a sharper pain

Mutes all torments and fears.

CYMBELINE

Beyond duty? obedience?

IMOGEN

Beyond hope and in despair, so beyond heaven's grace.

CYMBELINE

You could have had the sole son of my queen!   80

IMOGEN

I'm blessed that I could not! I chose an eagle,

And did avoid a pigeon.

CYMBELINE

You took a beggar, would have made my throne

Into a vulgar nest.

IMOGEN

No, instead I added   85

A luster to it.

CYMBELINE

Oh you vile one!

IMOGEN

Sir,

It is your fault that I have loved Posthumus:

You raised him as my playmate, and he is   90

A man worth any woman: he pays double

What he should pay for me.

CYMBELINE

What? Are you mad?

IMOGEN

Almost, sir: gods, let me be born again

A herdsman's daughter, and my Leonatus   95

Our neighbor-shepherd's son!

CYMBELINE

You foolish thing! —

The Queen re-enters

They were together again: you've refused
To honor our command. Take her away,
And lock her up.   100

QUEEN

I implore your patience. (*to Imogen*) Hush,
Dear lady daughter, hush! — Sweet sovereign,
Leave us to ourselves, and try to find some comfort
In your counselors' advice.

CYMBELINE

No, let her suffer,   105
Her hearts-blood draining out one drop a day
Until this folly kills her.

Cymbeline and the Lords exit

QUEEN (*if to Cymbeline*)

Come now! You must relent.

(*or, if it's to Imogen*)

Come now! You must obey.

Pisanio enters

Here is your servant. What now, sir? What news?   110

PISANIO

Lord Cloten, your son, threatened my master, Posthumus.

QUEEN

Ha!
No harm is done, I trust?

PISANIO

There could have been,
If my master'd been fighting, not just playing,   115
And cared enough to be angry: they were parted
By nearby gentlemen.

QUEEN

I am glad for that.

IMOGEN

Your son flatters my father, plays his part well,

To threaten a poor exile. Oh brave sir!   120

I wish they were on a real battlefield,

And I there with my sword, ready to stab

The first to run. Why did you leave your master?

PISANIO

He ordered me to, and refused to allow me

To bring him to the harbor: left these notes   125

With orders that I follow your commands

When you should wish to use me.

QUEEN

He has been

Your faithful servant: I'd dare stake my honor

That he'll remain so.   130

PISANIO

I humbly thank your Highness

QUEEN (*to Imogen*)

Come, walk with me.

IMOGEN (*to Pisanio*)

In half an hour or so, come speak with me;

For now, you must go see my lord board ship.

They exit

ACT 1 ♦ SCENE 3

THE SAME

Cloten and two Lords enter

FIRST LORD

Sir, I would advise you to change your shirt; the rigors of
action have made you reek like rotting remains: where air
comes out, air comes in: and there are no scents outside as
invigorating as those you vent.

9

CLOTEN

If my shirt were bloody, then I'd change it. Have I hurt him? 5

SECOND LORD (*aside*)

No, I swear: not even his patience.

FIRST LORD

Hurt him? If he's not hurt, then his body's a holy carcass.
Why it's a thoroughfare for steel, if it's not hurt.

SECOND LORD (*aside*)

His own sword was evading arrest, so it took the back streets.

CLOTEN

The villain could not stand his ground. 10

SECOND LORD (*aside*)

No, but he kept fleeing forward, toward your face.

FIRST LORD

Stand his ground? You have enough ground of your own: but
he even added to your holdings, gave you some land.

CLOTEN

I wish they had not come between us.

SECOND LORD (*aside*)

So do I, to measure this fool six feet under. 15

CLOTEN

How can she love this oaf, and refuse me!

SECOND LORD (*aside*)

If it's a sin to make an honest choice, she is damned.

FIRST LORD

Sir, as I always tell you, her beauty and her brain don't go together.
She shines bright to the eye, but the reflection of her wit is dim.

SECOND LORD (*aside*)

She won't shine on fools, in case she's hurt by the reflection. 20

CLOTEN

Come on, I'm going to my room. I wish some pain had been
    inflicted!

SECOND LORD (*aside*)

I only wish for this ass's fall, which is no great pain.

CLOTEN (*to Second Lord*)

You'll go with us?

FIRST LORD

I'll attend your lordship.

CLOTEN (*to Second Lord*)

No, come, let's go together. 25

SECOND LORD

Fine, my lord.

They exit

ACT 1 ◆ SCENE 4

THE SAME

Imogen and Pisanio enter

IMOGEN

What was the last thing Posthumus said to you?

Tell me, Pisanio —

PISANIO

It was, his queen, his queen!

IMOGEN

Then waved his handkerchief?

PISANIO

And kissed it, madam. 5

IMOGEN

Oh lifeless linen, happier still than I!

And that was all?

PISANIO

No, madam: for as long

As with my eyes or ears I managed to

Distinguish him from others, he stayed above 10

The deck, waving his glove, or handkerchief,

11

Or hat, the fits and turmoil of his mind
Expressing best how slowly his soul sailed on,
How swift his ship.

IMOGEN

You should have kept looking 15
'Til he was small as a wren.

PISANIO

Ma'am, so I did.

IMOGEN

I would never have blinked — let my eyes crack dry
Gazing at him, 'til he had melted from
The smallness of a gnat, into air: and then 20
Have looked away, and wept. But, good Pisanio,
When will we hear from him?

PISANIO

Be assured, madam,
The first chance that he has.

IMOGEN

I did not finish my farewell, but had 25
Such tender things to say: before I could tell him
How I would think of him at certain hours,
Such thoughts and such: or I could make him swear
The "bellas" of Italia would not betray
My place in his heart, and his honor: before I could 30
Give him that parting kiss, which I had set
Between two words like charms, in comes my father,
And like the tyrannous cold breath of the north,
Shakes th' blossoms from our buds.

A Lady enters

LADY

The Queen, madam, 35
Desires your Highness's company.

IMOGEN (*to Pisanio*)

Those things I bid you do, see that they're done —

I will go to the Queen.

PISANIO

Madam, I will.

They exit

ACT 1 ◆ SCENE 5

ROME. PHILARIO'S HOUSE.

Philario, Iachimo, a Frenchman, a Dutchman, and a Spaniard enter

IACHIMO

Believe it sir, I have seen this Posthumus in Britain; he was
then a rising star, expected to prove as worthy as they now
claim he is. But I could not locate in him anything to admire.

PHILARIO

You speak of him when he was less adorned than he is now
with that which enriches him inside and out.   5

FRENCHMAN

I saw him in France: we have very many men strong enough
to behold the sun like an eagle, with eyes as firm as he.

IACHIMO

This business of marrying his king's daughter, in which we
must weigh him more by her value than his own, exaggerates
his reputation beyond his worth.   10

FRENCHMAN

And then his banishment.

IACHIMO

Right, and the sympathy of those who mourn their lamen-
table separation, inflates his reputation further, even if just
to defend her judgment, which any weak attack could easily
crush, for accepting a beggar already so low. But how is it that   15
he comes to stay with you? How did he steal your friendship?

13

PHILARIO

His father and I were soldiers together, and I have often owed him no less than my life. — Here comes that same Briton!

Posthumus enters

I beg you all to introduce yourself to this gentleman, whom I commend to you as a noble friend of mine. 20

FRENCHMAN

Sir, we were acquainted in Orléans.

POSTHUMUS

Since when I've been in your debt for generosity, which I could never repay, and still owe to you.

FRENCHMAN

Sir, you overrate my measly kindness: I was glad to reconcile you and my countryman: it would have been a pity for you to 25 duel over such a slight and trivial matter.

POSTHUMUS

Beg your pardon, sir, I was then a young traveler, but even now, with my mended judgment (if I may say it is mended), my quarrel was not exactly slight.

FRENCHMAN

Indeed it was, too slight to be decided by swords, and by two 30 such men.

IACHIMO

Are we impolite to ask what caused the conflict?

FRENCHMAN

Not at all, I think. It was much like the argument which we fell into last night, each of us lavishly praising our beloved *mesdemoiselles* back home; this gentleman at the time vouch- 35 ing that his lady was more lovely, virtuous, wise, chaste, faithful, praiseworthy, and less temptable to seduction than any of the most extraordinary ladies in France.

IACHIMO

That lady does not exist; or this gentleman's opinion, is by
now quite out-of-date.   40

POSTHUMUS

Her virtue remains unchanged, as does my mind.

IACHIMO

You cannot claim she so outshines ours of Italy.

POSTHUMUS

Provoke me as far as the French did, and I will not reduce
her worth.

IACHIMO

If she outclassed others I have seen, as that diamond of yours   45
outlusters many I've beheld, I would believe that she might
shine brighter than many: but I've not yet seen the most precious diamond that is, nor you the lady.

POSTHUMUS

I praised her as I rated her: just as I do my stone.

IACHIMO

What do you esteem its worth at?   50

POSTHUMUS

More than the world possesses.

IACHIMO

Either your unparagoned mistress is dead, or she's outvalued
by a bauble.

POSTHUMUS

You are mistaken: one might be sold or given; the other is not
a thing for sale, and is only the gift of the gods.   55

IACHIMO

Which the gods have given you?

POSTHUMUS

Which by their graces I will keep.

IACHIMO

You may hold the title to that land as yours: but you know
that strange fowl do alight on neighboring ponds. Your ring
may be stolen too: so too, the jewel you estimate priceless, for 60
one is weak, the other prone to accident; a cunning thief, or
a courtier accomplished in certain arts, might risk trying to
win both the first one and the last.

POSTHUMUS

Your Italy contains no courtier accomplished enough to van-
quish the honor of my mistress, if you call her weak in the 65
keeping or loss of her honor: I have no doubt that you know
many thieves; nevertheless, I do not fear for my ring.

PHILARIO

Let us end this here, gentlemen.

POSTHUMUS

Sir, with all my heart. This worthy signor, I thank him, does
not treat me like a stranger; he acts quite familiar from the 70
start.

IACHIMO

With just five times this much talk, I could gain ground on
your mistress; push her back even to the point of yielding, if
I had the access and opportunity to befriend her.

POSTHUMUS

No, no. 75

IACHIMO

I'll stake half of my estate on this, if you will stake your ring,
which in my opinion somewhat overvalues it: but I make my
wager more against your confidence than her reputation.
And to prevent personal affront to you, I'll dare attempt it on
any lady in the world. 80

POSTHUMUS

You are greatly deceived in your opinion, which is too bold, and no doubt you'll receive what you deserve for your efforts.

IACHIMO

What's that?

POSTHUMUS

Rejection: though your attempt (as you call it) deserves
more; a punishment too.   85

PHILARIO

Gentlemen, enough of this, it flared up too suddenly, let it die
as it was born, and treat each other more civilly.

IACHIMO

I wish I'd staked my whole estate and my neighbor's too, on
the proof of what I've said!

POSTHUMUS

What lady would you choose to ambush?   90

IACHIMO

Yours, whose faithfulness you think stands in such safety. I
will lay down ten thousand ducats to your ring, betting that,
with just your letter of introduction to the court, I'll bring
back that honor of hers which you imagine so well-guarded.

POSTHUMUS

I will wager against your gold, more gold to match it: my   95
ring, which I treasure as much as my finger — it's part of it.

IACHIMO

You can buy the purest lady's flesh, at a million an ounce,
but you can't protect it from stain; but I see you have some
religion in you, since you fear.

POSTHUMUS

The goodness of my mistress exceeds the hugeness of your   100
vulgarity. I dare you to this match: here's my ring.

PHILARIO

I will not allow this wager.

IACHIMO

By the gods, the game is on. If I bring you insufficient proof
that I have possessed the most precious bodily part of your
mistress, my ten thousand ducats are yours, as is your dia- 105
mond too. So if I return having left her with the honor that
you so trust in, then she your jewel, this your jewel, and my
gold are yours: as long as you've provided me your introduction to the court, to ensure I'll be received there.

POSTHUMUS

I embrace these conditions, add them to the agreement. 110
Only, you must agree to this: if you set off to conquer her,
and prove to me that you have prevailed, I will no longer
be your enemy; she is not worth our debate. If she remains
unseduced, then, for your foul opinion, and for the assault
you have made on her chastity, you will answer me with your 115
sword.

IACHIMO

Give me your hand, we are bound: we'll have these things set
down by lawful counsel, and I'll leave straight away for Britain, before this bargain catches cold and starves.

POSTHUMUS

Agreed. 120

Posthumus and Iachimo exit

FRENCHMAN

Will they stick to it, you think?

PHILARIO

Signor Iachimo will not back away. Come please, let's follow
them.

They exit

ACT 1 ♦ SCENE 6

BRITAIN. CYMBELINE'S PALACE.

The Queen and Cornelius enter

QUEEN

Now master doctor, have you brought those drugs?

CORNELIUS

As your Highness requested, yes: here, madam:

(presenting a small box)

But might you tell me, your grace, without offense,

(My conscience urges me to ask) why you have

Ordered me to make these poisonous compounds,   5

Which usher one towards a long, drawn-out death:

But even though slow, deadly.

QUEEN

Doctor, I'm shocked

You ask me such a question. Haven't I been

Your faithful pupil? Have you not taught me how   10

To make perfumes? Distill? Preserve? So well,

That our great king himself begs me to give him

More of my blends? Having progressed so far

(Unless you think me evil) isn't it

Appropriate that I expand my knowledge in   15

Other experiments? I'll test the strength

Of these compounds of yours on creatures that

Are not even worth hanging (but no human)

To test the power they have, then administer

Aids to reduce their effects, and this way learn   20

The assets and the qualities of each.

CORNELIUS

Your Highness

Will only harden your own heart doing this:

Besides, witnessing these effects will be

19

Both disagreeable and foul.   25
QUEEN
    Oh do not worry.
(*aside*)
    Here comes a fawning scoundrel, he's the one
    I'll work on first: he's pulling for his master,
    And enemy to my son. (*to Pisanio*) How are you, Pisanio?
    Doctor, your service for this time is ended,   30
    Feel free to go.
(*to Pisanio*)
    Wait now, a word.
CORNELIUS (*aside*)
    I do not like her. She thinks that she has
    Strange lingering poisons: but I see her intent,
    And will not trust one of her malice with   35
    So diabolical a drug. The one she has
    Will stupefy and dull senses awhile;
    Which first (perhaps) she'll try on cats and dogs,
    Then afterwards aim higher: but there is
    No danger in its masquerade of death,   40
    Just a paralysis of life-force for a while,
    Only to wake more fresh. She will be fooled
    With false effects: And I will be more honest
    Acting false with her.
QUEEN
    No further service, doctor,   45
    Until I send for you.
CORNELIUS
    I humbly take my leave.
                    Cornelius exits
QUEEN (*to Pisanio*)
    She's weeping still, you say? Go do your work:

And when you tell me that she loves my son,
I'll be the first to tell you then, that you're   50
As great as your own master: greater, for
His fortunes have no voice, and his name — "Posthumus" —
Is gasping for a breath. He can't return,
Nor stay on where he is.

(The Queen drops the box. Pisanio takes it up.)

      You don't know   55
What you pick up: but take it for your labor:
It is a thing I made, which five times now
Has rescued the King from death. I do not know
A thing more curative. No, take it, please;
A small sampling of more rewards that I   60
Intend to give you. Tell your mistress how
Her situation stands: do it in your words;
Think what you'd gain to change your loyalties;
I'll sway the King to give you any promotion
You might desire. Think on my words.   65

      Pisanio begins to exit

QUEEN *(aside)*

 A sly and loyal knave.
 He won't be moved. But what I gave him,
 If he then drinks it, will eliminate
 The last ambassador for her love: and then,
 Unless her spirits lift, she'll surely choose   70
 To taste it too.

(to Pisanio)

 Fare you well, Pisanio;
 Think on my words.

      Queen exits

PISANIO

 That I will do:

21

But when to my good lord I prove untrue, 75
I'll hang myself: that's all I'll do for you.

He exits

ACT 1 ◆ SCENE 7

THE SAME

Imogen enters alone

IMOGEN

A father cruel, a stepmother false,
A foolish suitor to a wedded lady,
Whose husband has been banished: — Oh, that husband,
Supreme crown of my grief! and the aggravation
Of it, endless! If thieves had stolen me, 5
Like my brothers, I'd be happy: but misery
Awaits all grand desires. Blessed be those who
Being humble, have their simple, honest wants
Which give sweet comfort. — Agh! Who can this be?

Pisanio and Iachimo enter

PISANIO

Madam, a noble gentleman of Rome, 10
Comes from my lord with letters.

IACHIMO

Madam, change
Your look, the worthy Leonatus is now safe
And sends his dearest affection.

He presents a letter

IMOGEN

Thanks, good sir: 15
You're kindly welcome.

IACHIMO (*aside*)

How lustrous all of her that sees the sun!
If inside she's decorated with as rich

A mind, she is the one true Phoenix; and I
Have lost the wager. Boldness, be my friend!   20
IMOGEN (*reads*)

"*He is one of the noblest reputation, to whose kindnesses I am
most deeply tied. Treat him accordingly, as you value your truest Leonatus.*"

That's all I'll read aloud.
But even the very middle of my heart   25
Is warmed by the rest, and drinks it gratefully.
You are as welcome, worthy sir, as I
Have words to welcome you, and this will show
In all that I can do.
IACHIMO

Thanks, madam.   30
(*to Pisanio*)

Excuse me, sir,
Please ask my man to wait just where I left him:
He's foreign and temperamental.
PISANIO

I was going,
Sir, to welcome him.   35

Pisanio exits

IMOGEN

Did you find my Lord well? How is his health?
IACHIMO

Well, madam.
IMOGEN

Are his spirits high? I hope he finds some joy.
IACHIMO

Extremely high: he's amiable with all,
So cheerful and so fond of games: he's called   40
The British reveler.

IMOGEN

When he was here
He tended more towards sadness, and often
Not knowing why.

IACHIMO

I never saw him sad. 45
There is a Frenchman who it seems much loves
A Gallian girl at home. His sighs belch from him
Like a hot furnace; while the jolly Brit
(Your lord, I mean) laughs loud and free: cries "Oh,
My sides split just to think that men, who know 50
What "Woman" is — what she can't help but be —
Will waste their free days waiting for their own
Most certain bondage?"

IMOGEN

That's what my Lord says?

IACHIMO

Ay, madam, with his eyes flooding with laughter: 55
It entertains us all to be near him
And hear him mock the Frenchman: but heaven knows
Some men commit worse offenses.

IMOGEN

Not he, I hope.

IACHIMO

Not he: although the gifts the gods endowed him with 60
Could be less squandered, for his bounty's lush:
While it inspires awe in me, it inspires
Some pity too.

IMOGEN

What do you pity, sir?

IACHIMO

Two creatures, with all my heart. 65

IMOGEN

Am I one, sir?

You look at me: do you see some broken thing

That deserves pity?

IACHIMO

How deplorable!

To hide from the sun's radiance, and find comfort   70

With a spent candle in the dark?

IMOGEN

I beg you, sir,

Respond with more directness to the questions

I ask of you. Why do you pity me?

IACHIMO

That others do —   75

(I was about to say) enjoy your — But

It is the business of the gods to avenge it,

Not mine to speak of it.

IMOGEN

But you seem to know

Something of me, or what concerns me; please —   80

Since worrying that things go badly can hurt more

Than knowing that they do — reveal to me

That which you spur, then stop.

IACHIMO

Had I this cheek

To bathe my lips upon: this hand, whose touch   85

(Whose every touch) would force the feeler's soul

To an oath of loyalty: this object, which

Imprisons the wild motion of my eye,

Fixating it just here; should I (damn me)

Slobber on lips as trafficked as the stairs   90

Of Jupiter's temple: fondle and grab hands

25

Made hard with hourly tricks? No — it would be right
For all the plagues of hell to rise together
And confront this obscene sight.

IMOGEN

My lord, I fear,   95
Has forgot Britain.

IACHIMO

And himself. It's not I,
Nor my need to share this knowledge that declares
His most despicable change: but it's your Grace
That from my own mute conscience to my tongue   100
Charms out this foul report.

IMOGEN

Let me hear no more.

IACHIMO

Oh dearest soul: your cause pierces my heart
With pity enough to make me sick! Be revenged,
Or she that bore you was no queen, and you   105
Prove worthless of your ancestry.

IMOGEN

Revenged!
How should I be revenged? If this is true,
(And my heart reminds me that both my ears
Must not in haste condemn him) if it's true,   110
How should I be revenged?

IACHIMO

If he made me
Lie like Diana's virgins, between cold sheets,
While he straddles new strumpets every night,
Despite your love, drawing from your purse — revenge it.   115
I dedicate myself to your sweet pleasure,
More noble than that deserter of your bed,

And will stay loyal to your affections, both
Discreet and true.

IMOGEN

Come now, Pisanio! 120

IACHIMO

Let me offer my service on your lips.

IMOGEN

Get out! And damn my ears for listening
To you for far too long. If you were honorable
You would have told this tale to do what's right,
Not for the end you seek, so base, so foul. 125
You wrong a gentleman who is as far
From your description as you are from honor,
And solicit here a lady that disdains
You, and the devil too. Come now, Pisanio!
The King, my father, shall be well informed 130
Of your assault: Come now, Pisanio!

IACHIMO

O happy Leonatus! I must say:
The credit that you give your worthy lady
Deserves your trust. Bless you, and live long!
Give me your pardon. 135
I spoke like this to see if your sacred pledge
Was deeply rooted, but now I'll restore your Lord
To his true self again (that is, the one
Who's pure and faithful: such a holy sorcerer
That none can help being lured by his enchantments: 140
Half all men's hearts are his).

IMOGEN

You make amends.

IACHIMO

Among men, he's like a god. Please don't be angry,

Most mighty Princess, that I have dared to test
What your response might be to this false tale,   145
Which only has confirmed your excellent judgment
In choosing such a peerless gentleman,
Who you know cannot sin. The love I bear him
Spurred me to challenge you, but unlike others,
The gods made you steadfast. I beg your pardon.   150

IMOGEN

All's well, sir: I offer you all I have at court.

IACHIMO

My humble thanks. I had almost forgot
To entreat your grace for a favor; it's quite small,
Yet important to your lord.

IMOGEN

Please, what is it?   155

IACHIMO

Some dozen of us Romans, and your lord
(The best feather of our wing) have pooled our funds
To buy a present for the emperor:
Jewels of exquisite form, whose value is great,
And I am anxious, being a stranger here,   160
To have them safely stored: might it please you
To take them in protection?

IMOGEN

Willingly:
I'd pawn my honor for their safety, since
My lord's invested in them; I will keep them   165
In my bedchamber.

IACHIMO

They are in a trunk
Which my servants are watching: I'll be so bold
To send them to you, only for tonight:

I must sail back to-morrow. 170

IMOGEN

Oh, no, no.

IACHIMO

I fear so: or I'll fall short of my word

By lengthening my stay.

IMOGEN

Send your trunk to me, it shall be kept safe,

And faithfully given back: you're very welcome. 175

They exit

ACT 2 ◆ SCENE 1

BRITAIN. IN FRONT OF CYMBELINE'S PALACE.

Cloten and the two Lords enter

CLOTEN

Has there ever been a man with luck like mine? I'd bet a hundred pounds on that ball: and then that damned monkey son of a whore had to scold me for swearing.

FIRST LORD

And what did he get for it? You cracked his head open with your ball.   5

SECOND LORD *(aside)*

If his brains were like the one's who cracked it, they'd have run out fast.

CLOTEN

When a gentleman is inclined to swear, no stander-by has a right to cut off his curses. Right?

SECOND LORD

No, my lord; *(aside)* Nor to crop an ass's ears.   10

CLOTEN

Bastard dog! I wish his rank equaled mine!

SECOND LORD *(aside)*

To have smelled like a fool.

CLOTEN

I'd rather not be as noble as I am: they don't dare fight with me, because of the Queen, my mother: every vulgar lug gets his bellyful of fighting, and I, being superior, can only strut   15
up and down like a cock.

SECOND LORD *(aside)*

You are cock and "eggless" capon too, crowing "cock!" with your fool's cap on.

CLOTEN

What did you say?

SECOND LORD

It is not fitting for your lordship to take on every character 20
that you give offense to.

CLOTEN

No, I know that: but it is fitting for me to inflict offense upon
inferiors.

SECOND LORD

Ay, only fitting for your lordship …

FIRST LORD

Did you hear about the new foreigner that's come to court 25
tonight?

CLOTEN

A stranger, and I know nothing of it?

SECOND LORD (*aside*)

He's a strange fellow himself, and doesn't know it.

FIRST LORD

It's an Italian who has come; they say he's one of Posthumus
Leonatus's friends. 30

CLOTEN

Posthumus? A banished scoundrel; and he's one too, who-
ever he is. Is it fitting for me to take a look at him? It won't
diminish my dignity?

SECOND LORD

It cannot be diminished, my lord.

CLOTEN

Not easily, I think. Come, I'll go see this Italian: what I have 35
lost today at bowling, I'll win from him tonight. Come on:
go.

SECOND LORD

I will follow your lordship.

ACT 2 ♦ SCENE 1

Cloten and the First Lord exit

That such a crafty devil as is his mother
Should give the world this ass! A woman with   40
A brain that pierces through all, and her son
Can't subtract two from twenty, try as he might,
And end up with eighteen. Oh poor Princess,
You divine Imogen, what you've endured!
May the gods hold firm   45
Your precious honor's walls, and keep upright
That temple — your fair mind — so you might stand
To enjoy your banished lord and this great land!

He exits

ACT 2 ♦ SCENE 2

IMOGEN'S BEDCHAMBER

A trunk lies in one corner. Imogen is in her bed.

A Lady enters

IMOGEN

Who's there? My woman Helen?

LADY

To serve you, madam.

IMOGEN

What time is it?

LADY

Almost midnight, madam.

IMOGEN

I have read three hours, then: my eyes are weak.   5
Fold down the page where I have stopped: to bed.
Do not remove the candle, leave it burning:
And if you manage to rise by four o'clock,
Please call to me. Sleep's seized my body and soul.

The Lady exits

33

I entrust myself to your protection, gods: 10
From fairies and the tempters of the night.

She sleeps. Iachimo emerges from the trunk.

IACHIMO

The crickets sing, and man's overworked mind
Repairs itself by rest. Oh Venus —
How perfectly you suit your bed! Fresh lily!
Unblemished as the sheets! How I long to touch! 15
A kiss, one kiss! Oh rubies beyond compare,
How exquisite their caress: it's her breathing
That so perfumes the chamber. But to my plan.
To observe the chamber: I'll write all of it down:
Such and such pictures: there, the window: those 20
Her bed's adornments; drapery, carved mantel,
Why, such and such: and telling such a story.
Ah, but some natural details of her body
Would bear witness, and enrich my account
More than ten thousand petty furnishings. 25
Oh sleep, mimic death: lie heavy upon her,
And numb her senses like a figure of stone,
Lying quietly in a chapel. Come off, come off;

(taking off her bracelet)

As slippery as the Gordian knot was tangled.
It's mine, to testify for outside eyes, 30
As strongly as his doubting heart inside,
Driving her lord insane. By her left breast
A mole with five spots: like the crimson drops
In the base of a cowslip blossom. Oh this secret
Will make him think I've picked the lock, and taken 35
The treasure of her honor. No more: what for?
Why should I write this down, that's riveted,
Screwed to my memory? I have enough:

Back to the trunk again, and shut it tight.
Swift, swift, you dragons of the night, that dawn's   40
New light may wake the raven! I hide in fear;
Though she's a heavenly angel, hell is here.

(the clock strikes)

One, two, three: time's up, time's up!

He hides in the trunk

ACT 2 ◆ SCENE 3

THE PALACE

Cloten and the Lords enter

FIRST LORD

Your lordship is the most patient man who ever lost, the
most cool that ever threw snake eyes.

CLOTEN

It chills any man to lose.

FIRST LORD

But you are so hot and passionate when you win.

CLOTEN

Winning will get any man's courage up. If I could get this   5
foolish Imogen, then I'd have plenty of gold. It's almost
morning, isn't it?

FIRST LORD

Day, my lord.

CLOTEN

I wish these musicians would come: I've been advised to play
her music in the mornings, they say it will penetrate.   10

The Musicians enter

Come on, tune up: if you can penetrate her with your finger-
ing, good: we'll try with tongue too: if nothing works, then
let her be, but I'll never give up. First, a very fancy, elabo-
rate thing; then, a wonderful sweet ditty with impressively

copious words, and then let her contemplate. 15

(*singing*)

Hark, hark, the lark at heaven's gate sings,
And Phoebus starts to arise,
His steeds go to drink at that spring
That on cupped blossoms lies;
And sleeping marigolds start to open their golden eyes 20
With everything that's pretty, my lady sweet, arise:
Arise, arise!

So, get gone now: if this penetrates, I will judge your music
better, if it doesn't, there is a defect in her ears.

The Musicians exit

SECOND LORD

Here comes the King. 25

CLOTEN

I am glad I was up so late, for that's the reason I am up so
early: he cannot help but interpret this service I have done in
a fatherly fashion.

Cymbeline and the Queen enter

Good morning to your majesty, and to my gracious mother.

CYMBELINE

Are you waiting by our stern daughter's door? 30
Will she not come out?

CLOTEN

I have lain into her with musics, but she grants me no notice.

CYMBELINE

The exile of her plaything is too new,
She still cannot forget him, some more time
Must wear out the fading imprint of his memory 35
And then she's yours.

QUEEN

You are beholden to the King,

Who loses no opportunity to commend
You to his daughter: obey her in everything
Except when she commands you to be gone: 40
Then, act insensible.

CLOTEN

Insensible? Me?

A Messenger enters

MESSENGER

If you please, sir, ambassadors from Rome:
Their head is Caius Lucius.

CYMBELINE

A worthy fellow,   45
Though he may come now with an angry purpose;
But that's no fault of his: we must receive him
According to the honor of he who sent him. Dear son,
When you have said good morning to your mistress,
Come to the Queen and us; we shall have need   50
To use you with this Roman. Come, our queen.

All but Cloten exit

CLOTEN

If she is up, I'll speak with her: if not,
Let her lie still, and dream. Excuse me, hey!

He knocks. A Lady enters.

LADY

Who's there that knocks?

CLOTEN

A gentleman.   55

LADY

No more?

CLOTEN

Yes, and a gentlewoman's son.

LADY

That's more

Than some who dress as expensively as you

Can justly brag of. What does my lord desire?   60

CLOTEN

Your lady's person, is she ready?

LADY

Yes,

To stay in her room.

CLOTEN

There is gold for you,

Let me buy your good word.   65

LADY

To sell you my good name? Or to describe you

With words good for that purpose? The Princess!

The Lady exits. Imogen enters.

CLOTEN

Good morning, fairest sister — your sweet hand.

IMOGEN

Good morning, sir. You pay out too much effort

Only to purchase trouble: the thanks I give   70

Are just to tell you I'm bankrupt of thanks,

And scarce can spare them.

CLOTEN

Still I swear I love you.

IMOGEN

Just saying so would carry the same weight:

If you still swear, your recompense is still   75

That I pay no attention.

CLOTEN

That's no answer.

IMOGEN

    I would not speak at all, but then you'd take

    My silence as consent. Please let me be.

CLOTEN

    To leave you in your madness would be a sin,   80

    I will not.

IMOGEN

    Fools cannot cure mad folks.

CLOTEN

    Do you call me fool?

IMOGEN

    As I am mad, I do:

    If you will leave me, I'll be mad no more,   85

    That cures us both. I am most sorry, sir,

    You do make me forget a lady's manners

    By being so verbal:learn now, and forever,

    That I, knowing my heart, do here pronounce,

    By its honest truth, I do not care for you,   90

    And am so close to lacking charity

    (To accuse myself) I hate you.

CLOTEN

    You sin against

    Obedience, which you owe your father; for

    The contract you allege with that foul wretch,   95

    One raised on charity, and fed with leftovers,

    With scraps of the court; it is no contract, none;

    You're heir to the crown, and so must not defile

    Its precious luster with a base slave,

    A derelict tramp, a servant's rags,   100

    A chore boy; even lower.

IMOGEN

    Profane cad,

If you were Jupiter's son, you'd be too base
To feed his dogs.

CLOTEN

Pestilence *rot* him! 105

IMOGEN

He'd meet no greater misfortune than to hear
His name pronounced by you. The lowliest garment
That ever embraced his body is more precious
Than all the hairs on your head, even if they were
Each changed into a man. Pisanio, come! 110

Pisanio enters

CLOTEN

"His garment?!" Now, the devil —

IMOGEN

Go immediately to see my woman, Dorothy.

CLOTEN

"His garment!"

IMOGEN

I'm tormented by a fool,
Alarmed, and angered worse. Go ask my woman 115
To search for a bracelet that accidentally
Has left my arm: it was your master's. I think
I saw it this morning: yes, I'm sure of it.
Last night it was on my arm; I kissed it:
I hope it hasn't flown away to tell my lord 120
That I kiss anyone but him.

PISANIO

It can't be lost.

IMOGEN

I hope not: go and search.

Pisanio exits

CLOTEN

You have abused me:

"His lowliest garment!"   125

IMOGEN

Yes, I said so, sir:

If you'll take up a lawsuit, call a witness.

CLOTEN

I will inform your father.

IMOGEN

Your mother too:

She's my good friend; and will assume, I hope,   130

Only the worst of me. So, I leave you, sir,

To the worst discontent.

She exits

CLOTEN

I'll be revenged:

"His lowliest garment!" Well.

He exits

ACT 2 ◆ SCENE 4

ROME. PHILARIO'S HOUSE.

Posthumus and Philario enter

POSTHUMUS

Don't worry, sir: I wish I were as sure

Of winning over the King as I am she'll keep

Her honor.

PHILARIO

What approaches have you made to him?

POSTHUMUS

Not any: I just wait for times to change,   5

Here shivering in my wintry state now and wishing

That warmer days would come.

41

PHILARIO

By now, your king
Has heard from great Caesar: for Caius Lucius
Performs his missions thoroughly. And I think   10
The King will grant the tribute: send debts owed,
Or he'll soon face our Romans, the memory of whom
Still causes him fresh grief.

POSTHUMUS

I do believe
That this will end in war, and you'll hear of   15
The legions that are now in Gallia landing
In our unflinching Britain before news
Of any tribute paid.

Iachimo enters

PHILARIO

Look! Iachimo!

POSTHUMUS

I hope the briefness of her answer spurred   20
The speediness of your return.

IACHIMO

Your lady,
Is one of the fairest that I have looked upon —

POSTHUMUS

The purest too, I might add.

IACHIMO

Here's letters for you.   25

POSTHUMUS

Their substance good, I trust.

IACHIMO

It's likely, yes.

PHILARIO

Was Caius Lucius in the British court

When you were there?

IACHIMO

He was expected then,   30
But not arrived.

POSTHUMUS

Sparkles this stone as usual, or is it
Too dull for you to flaunt?

IACHIMO

If I have lost it,
I would have happily lost its worth in gold —   35
I'd make a journey twice as far, to enjoy
A second night of such sweet shortness which
Was mine in Britain; for the ring is won.

POSTHUMUS

The stone's too hard to come by.

IACHIMO

Not at all,   40
Your lady being so easy.

POSTHUMUS

Sir do not jest
Because you lost. I hope you know that we
Must not continue friends.

IACHIMO

Good sir, we must   45
If you would keep our agreement. For I now
Profess myself the winner of her honor,
Together with your ring.

POSTHUMUS

If you can show me proof
That you have tasted her in bed, my hand   50
And ring are yours. If not, your foul opinion
Of her pure honor will cost you your sword,

43

Or win you mine.

IACHIMO

Sir, my evidence,

So intimate with truth, which I will keep to, 55

Will surely persuade you.

POSTHUMUS

Proceed.

IACHIMO

First, her bedchamber,

(Where I confess I slept not, but profess

What I had was worth watching) it was hung 60

With tapestries of silk and silver, showing

Proud Cleopatra, so lifelike —

POSTHUMUS

This is true:

And this you could have heard right here, from me,

Or from another. 65

IACHIMO

More particulars

Should verify my knowledge.

POSTHUMUS

So they should,

Or endanger your honor.

IACHIMO

The fireplace 70

Is on the south wall, and its carving shows

Chaste Diana, bathing: I have never seen

Figures more apt to come to life —

POSTHUMUS

Things like these

You also could have heard from someone else, 75

Since they are often spoken of.

IACHIMO

    The chamber's ceiling

    Is adorned with golden cherubs —

POSTHUMUS

    This ruins her honor?!

    Let's say for now you've seen all this (and let's   80

    Applaud your excellent memory); the description

    Of what is in her room by no means wins

    The wager you have made.

                Iachimo shows the bracelet

IACHIMO

    Then, if you're still

    Unmoved, and you don't mind, I'll show this jewel: see!   85

    And now back in the pocket: it must be married

    To your own diamond — I'll keep them.

POSTHUMUS

    Jove! —

    Once more let me look at it: is it that

    Which I left with her?   90

IACHIMO

    Sir (I thank her), that!

    She stripped it from her arm: I see her still:

    Her pretty act was worth more than her gift,

    And yet enriched it: she gave it to me,

    And said she prized it once.   95

POSTHUMUS

    Maybe she pluck'd it off

    To send to me.

IACHIMO

    She's written saying so? Has she?

POSTHUMUS

    O no, no, no, it's true. Here, take this too;

(gives him the ring)

> It curses me now like Medusa's stare,   100
> Kills me to look at it. The vows of women
> Are no more bound to where and whom they're made
> Than to their virtues, which is not at all.
> So false, so faithless!

PHILARIO

> Now have patience, sir,   105
> And take your ring again, it's not yet won:
> It may prove true that she had lost the bracelet: or
> Who knows if one of her women, being corrupted,
> Has stolen it from her?

POSTHUMUS

> Very true,   110
> I hope that's how he acquired it. Give it back,
> Provide me with some trait about her body
> More definite than this: for this was stolen.

Takes back ring

IACHIMO

> By Jupiter, I obtained it from her arm.

POSTHUMUS

> Listen, he swears: by Jupiter he swears.   115
> It's true, no, keep the ring, it's true: I am sure
> She would not lose it: her attendants are
> All pledged to her, and honest: — they induced to steal it?
> And by a stranger? No, he has seduced her:
> The token of her debauchery is this: 120

(holds out ring and gives it back)

> She has bought the name of whore, at a high price.
> There, take your fee. May all the fiends of hell
> Divide themselves between you both!

PHILARIO

    Be patient:

    This is not strong enough to be believed.   125

POSTHUMUS

    Never speak of it:

    She's been harnessed and ridden.

IACHIMO

    If you seek

    To satisfy your doubts, under her breast

    (Worthy of caressing) lies a mole, right proud   130

    Of its exquisite dwelling. Oh I swear

    I kissed it, and it filled me with urgent hunger

    To feed again, though full. You do remember

    This stain upon her?

POSTHUMUS

    Ay, and it confirms   135

    Another stain, as big as hell can hold,

    Even if it were all.

IACHIMO

    Will you hear more?

    Now I swear —

POSTHUMUS

    Don't swear.   140

    If you swear that you have not done it, you lie,

    And I will damn well kill you if you deny

    You made me a cuckold.

IACHIMO

    I'll deny nothing.

POSTHUMUS

    I wish that she were here, to rip her apart!   145

    I will go there and do it, in court, before

    Her father. I'll do something —

He exits

PHILARIO

You have won:

Let's follow him, and deflect the current rage

He aims against himself.   150

IACHIMO

With all my heart.

They exit

Posthumus re-enters

POSTHUMUS

Is there no way to birth men, without women

Adding their half? We are all bastards,

And that most venerable man, who I

Did call my father, was — who knows where? —   155

When I was coined. Some forger with his tool

Made me as a counterfeit: yet my mother seemed

A nonpareil to all: so does my wife,

Purer than any other. Oh vengeance, vengeance!

Me, she restrained from my own lawful pleasure,   160

And often asked for patience: did it with

A blushing modesty, a look so sweet

It could have warmed cold Saturn; to me she was

As chaste as untrod snow. Oh, all the devils!

This yellow Iachimo in an hour, was it?   165

Or less — immediately? What if he did not speak,

But like a gluttonous boar, true to himself,

Cried "Oh!" and mounted; found no opposition

Only the expected natural barrier which

She should guard from advances. Could I uproot   170

The woman's part in me — for there's no urge

That tends towards vice in man, that doesn't arise

From the woman's part: be it lying — see now —

The woman's: flattering, hers: deceiving, hers:
Lust and rank thoughts, hers, hers: revenges, hers: 175
Ambitions, envies, debaucheries, disdain,
Lewd longings, slanders, mercurial natures;
All faults of inconstancy, no, of hell, hers
In part, or all: definitely all. For even in vice
They are not constant, but are always changing   180
One vice, only a minute old, for one
Not half as old as that. I'll rail against them,
Detest them, curse them: yet it's wiser still
Hating truly, to pray they have their will:
The very devils couldn't plague them better.   185

He exits

ACT 3 ◆ SCENE 1

BRITAIN. CYMBELINE'S PALACE.

Cymbeline, Queen, Cloten, and Lords enter
with great pomp at one door.
At another, Caius Lucius and Attendants enter.

CYMBELINE

Now say, what is it Augustus Caesar requests?

LUCIUS

When Julius Caesar was in this Britain

And conquered it, Cassibelan, your uncle

(Famous in Caesar's praises, and no more

Than his great feats deserve it), to him,   5

And his successors, paid Rome a tribute tax,

Three thousand pounds a year; which (by you) lately

Has remained unpaid.

QUEEN

And, to kill the suspense:

Shall stay so always.   10

CLOTEN

There'll be many Caesars before another Julius: Britain's a
world by itself, and we won't pay a pound to wear our own
noses.

QUEEN

Remember, sir, my liege,

The kings, your ancestors, together with   15

The natural boldness of your isle. Here Caesar made

A kind of conquest, but did not brag that

He "Came, and saw, and overcame." With shame

(The first that ever touched him) he was carried

51

Away from our coast, twice beaten: and his ships   20
(Poor ignorant baubles) on our terrible seas
Were tossed like eggshells upon their swells, and cracked
As easily against our rocks.

CLOTEN

Come now, there's no more paying tribute: our kingdom is
stronger than it was at that time: and (as I said) there are no   25
more such Caesars.

CYMBELINE

Son, let your mother finish.

CLOTEN

Why tribute? Why should we pay tribute? If Caesar can
hide the sun from us with a blanket, or put the moon in his
pocket, we will pay him tribute for light: otherwise, sir, no   30
more tribute, please.

CYMBELINE

You must know,
'Til the oppressive Romans did extort
This tribute from us, we were free. Caesar's ambition
Put this hard yoke upon us; which to shake off   35
Suits well a warlike people, whom we reckon
Ourselves to be.

CLOTEN AND LORDS

We do.

CYMBELINE

Say then, to Caesar
Our ancestor was that Mulmutius who   40
Ordained our laws, which Caesar's sword has mangled
Beyond use; whose restoring and free exercise
Shall (by the power we hold) do our land well,
Though it inflame Rome's anger.

LUCIUS

    I am sorry, Cymbeline,   45

    That I must then pronounce Augustus Caesar

    (Caesar who's made more kings his servant than

    You have domestic officers) your enemy:

    Receive it from me, then. War and destruction

    In Caesar's name I now declare: expect   50

    Relentless fury. Your defiance set,

    I give my own thanks.

CYMBELINE

    You are welcome, Caius.

    Your Caesar knighted me; in youth I did

    Serve under him; with him I attained much honor,   55

    But his demanding it back from me by force,

    Requires defense at any cost.

LUCIUS

    Let the outcome speak.

CLOTEN

    His majesty bids you welcome. Remain with us a pleasant day

    or two, or longer: if you seek us afterwards on other terms,   60

    you'll find us ringed by a belt of salt-water: if you beat us out

    of it, it is yours: if you fall in the attempt, our crows' bellies

    will be the better for it: and there's an end.

LUCIUS

    So be it.

CYMBELINE

    I know your master's wish, and he knows mine: 65

    All that will come, we welcome.

They exit

ACT 3 ◆ SCENE 2

THE SAME

Pisanio enters, with a letter

PISANIO

What? Of adultery? Why don't you write then
What monster has accused her? Posthumus!
Oh master, what a strange infection
Has crept into your ear! What false Italian
(Proving their tongues as venomous as their poisons)   5
Infested your mistrustful ears? Disloyal? No.
She's punished for her honor, and endures,
More like a goddess than a wife, assaults that would
Defeat most people's virtue. Your mind, master,
Has sunk as low, compared to hers, as your fortunes   10
Once were. What's this? That I should murder her,
Because I vowed with love and truth to follow
And serve you faithfully? I, her? Her blood?
If that is what it means to do good service.
Then never call me serviceable.   15

(*reading*)

"Do it: the letter
That I have sent her will, by her own instructions,
Give you the opportunity." Oh damned paper!
Black as the ink that stains you! Unfeeling scrap,
Are you the accomplice in this act, though seeming   20
So unblemished and virgin-like? Look, here she comes.
I'll feign ignorance of what I am commanded.

Imogen enters

IMOGEN

What news, Pisanio?

PISANIO

Madam, here is a letter from my lord.

IMOGEN

    Who, your lord? that is my lord Posthumus! 25
    Oh you good gods,
    Let what is contained here taste of sweet love,
    Of my lord's health, and happiness: yet not
    Because we're apart; no, let that grieve him;
    Some griefs are treatable, that's one of them, 30
    The remedy is love: tell me he's happy
    In all but that! Oh let it be good news, gods!

(*she reads*)

    "Oh dearest of creatures, let your eyes give me new life. Be
    advised that I am in Wales at Milford-Haven: whatever your
    love tells you to do with this, follow it. Wishing you all happi- 35
    ness, and that your love may keep growing, he that remains
    loyal to his vow,
    Posthumus Leonatus."

    Oh, for a horse with wings! Did you hear, Pisanio?
    He is at Milford-Haven: read, and tell me 40
    How far it is. If one for petty business
    Might plod there in a week, why couldn't I
    Fly there in just a day? Then, true Pisanio,
    Who longs like me to see your lord; who longs
    (Oh withdraw that) not like me: who longs, 45
    But less intensely. O, not like me:
    For mine's beyond, beyond! How far is it
    To this same blessed Milford? And on the way
    Tell me how Wales was made so happy as
    To inherit such a haven. But, first of all, 50
    How can we steal away, how do we excuse
    The gap in time from when we first set off
    'Til we return: but first, how do we get there?
    We'll talk more of that later. Oh please speak,

How many miles can we cast off behind us   55
From hour to hour?

PISANIO

Sunrise to sundown, twenty's
Enough for you, madam: and too much too.

IMOGEN

Why, someone riding to his execution, man,
Would never go so slow: Go quick, find me   60
A riding-suit; no costlier than would fit
A landlord's housewife.

PISANIO

Madam, please reconsider.

IMOGEN

My eyes see straight on, man: not here, nor here,
Nor what comes next; those paths are filled with fog   65
That I cannot see through. Please go now, go,
Do as I asked you: there's no more to say:
For all that's in my sight is Milford's way.

They exit

ACT 3 ◆ SCENE 3

WALES. BEFORE THE CAVE OF BELARIUS.
Belarius, Guiderius, and Arviragus enter

BELARIUS

Too fine a day to stay indoors with those
Whose roof's as low as ours! Stoop, boys: this doorway
Instructs you how to adore the heavens; you bow
In worship of the holy morning. Kings'
Portals arch so high that giants strut through   5
Without even doffing their soaring turbans,
Or saying good morning to the sun. Hail, you fair heaven!

GUIDERIUS

Hail, heaven!

ARVIRAGUS

Hail, heaven!

BELARIUS

Now for our mountain sport, up to that hill!　　　　　　10

Your legs are young: I'll take the flat way. Think,

(When you're high enough to see me with crows' eyes),

About how that perspective makes things seem

Diminished or advantaged, and then remember

The tales I used to tell you of courts, of princes;　　　　15

Of the odd twists of war.

To understand this lets us learn from all we observe:

And often, to our comfort, we will find

The scaly beetle in its shell more safe

Than the great eagle flying high. Oh, this life　　　　　20

Is nobler than fawning on scolding lords:

Prouder than rustling in unpaid-for silk:

Expecting those who make your finery to bow to you,

Yet buying on credit: no life compared to ours.

GUIDERIUS

You speak from experience: we poor unfledged　　　　25

Have never flown beyond the view of the nest;

Don't know what the air's like far from home.

Maybe it's the best life (if quiet means best)

Sweeter to you, who's known a sharper one

And fitting for your brittle age; but for us　　　　　30

It is a cell of ignorance —

ARVIRAGUS

What should we talk about

When we're as old as you? When listening to

The rain and wind beat in a dark December?

57

What stories will we tell, cramped in our cave,   35
To talk away the freezing hours? None:
We have seen nothing: we're just beasts! We hunt
Like foxes, subtly, and warlike as the wolf,
For what we eat: we valiantly chase what flees:
Our cave we make into a cage, like captive birds,   40
And freely sing of bondage.

BELARIUS

Listen to you!
If you only knew the city's exploitations,
And had been pierced by them: the artifice
Of the court, as hard to leave as stay: if you try   45
To climb to the top you're sure to fall: or find
It's so slippery, the fear's as bad as falling:
Good actions are condemned: and what's worse,
Must curtsy at the blame. Oh boys, the world
Can read this story in me: my body's marked   50
By Roman swords; and once my reputation
Soared, with the illustrious. Cymbeline loved me,
And when they spoke of soldiers, my own name
Hung on everyone's lips: I was a tree
Whose boughs bent low with fruit. But in one night,   55
A storm, or robbery (call it what you will)
Shook down my ripe, sweet fruit, even my leaves,
And left me bare to the weather.

GUIDERIUS

Uncertain fortune!

BELARIUS

I had done nothing (as I've told you often)   60
But then two villains, whose false oaths condemned
My spotless honor, swore to Cymbeline
That I colluded with the Romans: so,

He banished me, and for these twenty years,
This rock, and these domains, have been my world   65
Where I have lived in honest freedom, paid
More pious debts to heaven than in all
My previous life. But up to the mountains!
This is not hunter's talk; the first that strikes
The deer will be the lord of the feast today,   70
The other two will serve him, and we won't
Fear poison, which lies everywhere in places
Of so-called higher status. Meet you in the valleys.

Guiderius and Arviragus exit

How hard it is to hide the sparks of Nature!
These boys could hardly know they're sons to the King,   75
Nor does Cymbeline dream that they're alive.
They think they're mine, and though they were raised humbly,
In this same cave they stoop in, their thoughts do hit
The roofs of palaces. This Polydore,
The heir of Cymbeline and Britain, who   80
The King, his father, called Guiderius — Jove!
When sitting on my three-legged stool I tell
My tales of warlike feats, his spirits fly out
Into my story: "My enemy fell like this,"
I say, "And here I laid my foot on his neck,"   85
So fast the princely blood flows in his cheek,
His body acts my words. The younger, Cadwal,
Once Arviragus, also takes a part,
Bringing my speech to life with his own fancies.
Oh Cymbeline, heaven and my conscience know   90
You banished me unjustly: at which point
I stole these children, three and two years old,
Hoping to wrest your heirs from you just as
You barred me from my lands. Euriphile,

You were their nurse, they took you for their mother, 95
And every day pay honor to your grave:
Myself, Belarius, whom they know as Morgan,
They take for their natural father. (*listens*) The game is on.

He exits

ACT 3 ◆ SCENE 4

COUNTRYSIDE NEAR MILFORD-HAVEN

Pisanio and Imogen enter

IMOGEN

You said when we dismounted that the place
Was close; my mother longed to see me born
Far less than I long now — Pisanio! man!
Where is Posthumus? What is on your mind
That makes you stare like that? Why sigh so sadly 5
From deep inside? Change your expression, please,
To look less terrifying, before wild panic
Attacks my steadier senses. What's the matter?
Why do you offer me that paper but
Offer no tender look? (*looks at letter*) My husband's hand? 10
Cursed Italy has out-crafted him
And he's in some dilemma. Speak, man, your words
May help to blunt some blow, which if I read
Would kill me on the spot.

PISANIO

I beg you, read; 15
And you'll see how I am (oh wretched thing)
No more than fortune's outcast.

IMOGEN (*reads*)

"Your mistress, Pisanio, has made my bed a harlot's play-
ground: the proofs of which have pierced my bleeding heart. I
speak not out of fear or flimsy guesses, but from proof as strong 20

as my grief, and my certainty is as sure as my revenge. That
part you, Pisanio, must perform for me, if your fidelity has
not been stained by the rupture of hers; let your own hands
take away her life. I will give you a chance to do so at Milford-
Haven: she has the letter I've written to lead her there: where,   25
if you fear to strike, and to prove to me with certainty it was
done, then you are flesh-peddler of her depravity, and to me
just as disloyal."

PISANIO

Why would I need to draw my sword? The paper
Has cut her throat already. No, it's slander,   30
Whose edge is sharper than the sword, whose tongue
Out poisons all of Egypt's snakes, whose breath
Flies on the rushing winds, and fills with lies
All corners of the world. Kings, queens, and states,
Old women, girls, death's secrets too: into all   35
The viper slander worms its way. Madam? —

IMOGEN

False to his bed? What is it to be false?
To lie, eyes open all night, and think of him?
To weep all day? And when asleep to dream
My love's in danger, and cry myself awake?   40
That's false to his bed?

PISANIO

Oh, my good lady!

IMOGEN

I false? Use your own judgment. Oh, Iachimo,
You had accused him of infidelity;
You then looked like a villain: now, I think,   45
You appear less twisted. Some florid Italian bird
(Adorned by paints, not nature) has ensnared him:
Poor me, I'm stale, a garment out of fashion,

And since I'm made of stuff too fine to scrap,
I must be split: — rip me to pieces — Oh,   50
Men's vows are women's traitors.

PISANIO

Dear madam, hear me.

IMOGEN (*to Pisanio*)

Come, you at least be true —
And do your master's bidding. When you see him,
Please testify to my obedience. Look,   55
I draw the sword myself: take it, and hit
The innocent mansion of my love, my heart:
Fear not, it's empty of all things but grief:
Your master is not there, and it was he
Who made it rich. Now do his bidding, strike.   60
Perhaps for a better cause you may be braver;
But now you seem a coward.

PISANIO

Get away, vile blade!
You will not damn my hand.

IMOGEN

Why, I must die: 65
And if I do not by your hand, you are
No servant of your master's. Against self-slaughter
There is a prohibition so divine
My weak hand shrinks from it. Look, here's my heart,
What is here?   70
The scriptures of the loyal Posthumus,
All turned to heresy? Get out, get out,
Corrupters of my faith!
And you, Posthumus, who roused and incited
My disobedience against the King, my father,   75
And make me cast aside the genteel courtship

Of my equals in rank, will one day find
Those acts of mine were no commonplace deeds,
But rare, extraordinary — and it grieves me
To think, when finally your sharp hunger's dulled   80
By she you feed on, how your memory
Will feel sharp pangs for me. Now do it, quick:
The lamb entreats the butcher.

PISANIO

Oh gracious lady:
Since I received orders to do this business   85
I have not slept one wink.

IMOGEN

Do it, and to bed then.

PISANIO

I'll stay awake 'til my eyes fall out.

IMOGEN

Then why
Did you set on this course? Why would you waste   90
So many miles, on this pretense? This place?
The perfect moment to act?

PISANIO

To win the time
To avoid this evil errand, during which
I've come up with another path for us: good lady,   95
Be patient, hear me.

IMOGEN

Talk your tongue off, speak:
I've heard I am a strumpet, and my ears
Struck with such slander cannot be wounded
Or pierced more deeply. Speak, then.   100

PISANIO

Well, madam,

I didn't think you'd go back.

IMOGEN

That's logical,

Bringing me here to kill me.

PISANIO

No, it's not so: 105

But if I'm wise as I am honest, then

My scheme could play out well: it must be that

My master's being exploited: some villain

(Yes, and a master in his art), has done you both

This hateful injury.   110

IMOGEN

Some Roman courtesan?

PISANIO

No, on my life:

I'll let him know that you are dead, and send him

Some bloody proof of it. For he has commanded

That I do so: you will be missed at court,   115

Which will confirm it further.

IMOGEN

Why, good man,

What will I do meanwhile? Where stay? How live?

What comfort's in my life now, when I am

Dead to my husband?   120

PISANIO

If you return to court —

IMOGEN

No court, no father, and no more to do

With that harsh, noble, simple nothing,

That Cloten, whose courtship has been to me

As frightening as a siege.   125

PISANIO

    If not at court,

    Then you cannot stay longer in Britain.

IMOGEN

    Where then?

    Does Britain own the shining sun? Day? Night?

    They're only in Britain? We're just a page in the book   130

    Of the world; a swan's nest in an endless pool —

    Life does exist beyond Britain.

PISANIO

    I am glad

    You think of other places: the ambassador,

    Caius Lucius the Roman, comes to Milford-Haven   135

    Tomorrow. Now, if you could just disguise

    That which, if it's revealed, endangers you

    (So it must stay hidden), you could tread a course

    Out in the open; maybe even near

    The residence of Posthumus.   140

IMOGEN

    Oh, for the chance of this,

    Though it may risk (but not yet kill) my honor,

    I'd hazard it!

PISANIO

    Well then, here's the plan:

    You must forget to be a woman: change   145

    Command into obedience: fear and demureness

    (That decorate all women, or better said,

    With grace they embody) into a jaunty courage,

    Ready to jest, quick-witted, saucy, and

    As quarrelsome as the weasel.   150

IMOGEN

    Now to the point:

I see the path you're heading down and am
Almost a man already.

PISANIO

First, dress like one.
Anticipating this, I already packed   155
(It's in my cloak-bag) jacket, stockings, hat,
All that goes with them: to noble Caius Lucius
Present yourself, offer your service: tell him
Of your talents; doubtless he'll take you in,
For he is honorable. As to how you'll live: 160
You have me, I have means, and I won't fail,
Not now, nor when you need them.

IMOGEN

You are all the comfort
The gods will feed me with. Now please, be off,
There's more to figure out: but I will rise   165
To this brave challenge, and endure it with
A prince's courage. Go now, please, away.

PISANIO

Here is a box — the Queen gave it to me.
What's in't is precious: if you're sick at sea,
Or queasy and ill on land, some drops of this   170
Will drive away malaise. Now go take cover,
And adapt to your new manhood: may the gods
Direct you the right way!

IMOGEN

Amen! And thank you.

They exit in opposite directions

ACT 3 ◆ SCENE 5

CYMBELINE'S PALACE

Cymbeline, Queen, Cloten, Lucius, and Lords enter

LUCIUS

Your Highness:

My emperor has written; I must leave,

And will be sorry to report you as

My master's enemy.

CYMBELINE

Our subjects, sir,   5

Will not be chained by him; and for ourself

To show less dignity than they do, would no doubt

Appear unkinglike.

LUCIUS

Aye. May I request

An escort on the road to Milford-Haven?   10

Madam, I wish you joy, your grace — (*to Cloten*) and you.

CYMBELINE

My lords, this is the very duty you are here for:

Honor our guest with our royal protection.

So farewell, noble Lucius.

LUCIUS (*to Cloten*)

Your hand, my lord.   15

CLOTEN

Now it seems friendly: but as of this moment

I wear it as your enemy.

LUCIUS

Sir, there's still

No winner to this contest. Fare you well.

CYMBELINE

My lords, do not yet leave the worthy Lucius,   20

'Til he's crossed the river Severn. All good fortune!

Lucius and Lords exit

QUEEN

He leaves here frowning: but it's to our credit

That we have given him cause.

CLOTEN

It's all the better!

And what your bravest Britons most desire.   25

CYMBELINE

Lucius has told the emperor already

What happened here. We must immediately

Ready our horsemen and our chariots.

QUEEN

It's no time to be idle —

We must attend to it urgently, with force.   30

CYMBELINE

We expected matters would fall out like this,

And so we are prepared. But, gentle Queen,

Where is our daughter? She did not appear

Before the Roman, nor greet us this morning

As proper daughters should. Tell her to come.   35

Messenger exits

QUEEN

Your Grace,

Do not speak sharply to her. She's delicate,

Such a fragile blossom that words are blows,

And blows death to her.

Messenger re-enters

CYMBELINE

Where is she?   40

MESSENGER

Please, my lord,

Her rooms are lock'd, and though we knocked and called,

We heard no answer to our clamorous noise.

QUEEN

My lord, when I last went to visit her,

She begged me to excuse the isolation 45

To which she is constrained by her ill health.

She'd asked me to convey this, but this Roman business

Made me forget. Blame me.

CYMBELINE

Her doors all locked?

Not seen lately? Please gods, let what I fear 50

Prove false!

He exits

QUEEN

Son hurry, follow the King.

CLOTEN

I haven't seen that man of hers, Pisanio,

Her old servant, for two whole days.

QUEEN

Look into it! 55

Cloten exits

Pisanio, always championing that Posthumus —

He has a drug of mine: (I pray his absence

Was caused by swallowing it!) For he

Believes it is a precious thing. But she —

Where has she gone? Perhaps despair has seized her: 60

Or, love's given her wings and she has flown

To her coveted Posthumus; well, she's gone,

To death or to dishonor, and my designs

Can make good use of either. She being down,

I have the placing of the British crown. 65

Cloten re-enters

What news, my son?

CLOTEN

It's certain she has fled:

Go in, cheer up the King; he rages, no one

Dares come near him.

QUEEN (*aside*)

All the better: may   70

Today's shock rob him of another day!

The Queen exits

CLOTEN

I love and hate Imogen: for she's fair and royal,

And all her parts are precious — so I love her,

But by rejecting me, and throwing those charms

To low Posthumus, she so discredits her sense   75

I will decide to hate her, no, what's more,

To be revenged upon her.

Pisanio enters

Who is here?

What are you scheming, sirrah? Come here: you knave!

Where is your lady? Tell me quick!   80

PISANIO

My lord!

CLOTEN

Where is your lady? Say, sly villain, or

I'll pry this secret from your heart, or slash

Your heart to find it. Is she with Posthumus?

PISANIO

How could she be with him? He is in Rome.   85

CLOTEN

Where is she, sir? Come nearer:

No further stalling: now come to the point,

PISANIO

Oh my all-worthy lord!

CLOTEN

> All-worthy villain,
> Speak, or your silence will suddenly become   90
> Your condemnation and your death.

PISANIO

> Then, sir:
> This paper here is all the story I know
> About her flight.

> *Presenting a letter to Cloten*

CLOTEN

> Let's see it: I will pursue her   95
> As far as Augustus' throne.

PISANIO (*aside*)

> It was this, or perish.
> She's far enough, and what he learns by this
> May take him on a detour, and not to her.

CLOTEN

> Hum!   100

PISANIO (*aside*)

> I'll tell Posthumus she's dead: Oh Imogen,
> Safe may you wander, safe return again!

CLOTEN

> Sirrah, is this letter true?

PISANIO

> Sir, I think so.

CLOTEN

> It is Posthumus' handwriting, I know it. Sirrah, if you'd like   105
> to end your villainous ways, you may do me some honorable
> service: that is, whatever villainy I ask you to do, perform it,
> straightaway and reliably, and you could count on my assets
> to assist you.

PISANIO

Fine, my good lord.   110

CLOTEN

Will you serve me?

PISANIO

Sir, I will.

CLOTEN

Give me your hand, here's your pay. Are any of your former
master's garments in your possession?

PISANIO

I have, my lord, in my room the same suit he wore when he   115
said farewell to my lady and mistress.

CLOTEN

The first task you'll do for me is to bring that suit here, let it
be your first assignment, go.

PISANIO

I will, my lord.

Pisanio exits

CLOTEN

Meet you at Milford-Haven! (I forgot to ask him one thing,   120
it'll come to me soon.) And right there, you villain Posthumus, I will kill you. I wish these garments would get here.
She said once (and I belch its bitterness from my heart) that
she respected even the lowliest garment of Posthumus more
highly than my naturally noble self; even with the added   125
adornment of my pedigree. Wearing that very same suit,
then, I will defile her: first kill him, and right in front of her;
then she'll see my valor, and be tormented by it. Once he's on
the ground, and once my lust has dined (which, as I say, I will
execute in the clothes that she so praised, to torture her) I'll   130
smack her back to court, kick her home again. She's rejoiced
in despising me, and I'll be gleeful in my revenge.

Pisanio re-enters, with the clothes

Are those the garments?

PISANIO

Yes, my noble lord.

CLOTEN

When did she set off to Milford-Haven?   135

PISANIO

She can't have gotten there yet.

CLOTEN

Bring this apparel to my bedroom, that is the second thing
that I have commanded you to do. The third is that you keep
silent as a mute about my plan. My revenge is to be found at
Milford: I wish I had wings to fly after it. Come with me, and   140
be loyal.

He exits

PISANIO

Give up my honor, you ask? Being true to you
Means to prove false, which I will never do,
To him that is the truest. To Milford go —
May you not find the one you seek. Flow, flow,   145
Heavenly blessings, onto her! May slowness
Thwart this fool's speed: toil be his recompense!

He exits

ACT 3 ◆ SCENE 6

WALES. IN FRONT OF THE CAVE OF BELARIUS.

Imogen enters, in boy's clothes

IMOGEN

I see a man's life is a tedious one,
I'm tired out: and for the last two nights
The ground has been my bed. I should be sick,
It's only my resolve that helps me: Milford,

When we peered at you from that mountain-top, 5
You were within my sights. Two beggars told me
I could not lose my way. Would poor folks lie,
Who suffer in misery already, knowing it's
A punishment, or test? Yes; it's no surprise,
When rich ones dodge the truth. Oh my dear lord, 10
You're one of the false ones! Now I think of you,
My hunger's gone: but just before, I was
Fainting for lack of food. — But what is this?
Here is a path to it: a rustic shelter:
I shouldn't call out; I don't dare call: but famine 15
Just when it overcomes you, makes you brave.
Hello! who's here?
If human, speak. If wild, take my life
Or help me. Hey! No answer? Then I'll enter.
I'll draw my sword; and if my enemy's 20
As scared of swords as I am, he won't look closely.
Send me a foe like that, oh gods!

She exits, into the cave

ACT 3 ◆ SCENE 7

THE SAME

Belarius, Guiderius, and Arviragus enter

BELARIUS

You, Polydore, as the best hunter today,
Will be Lord of the feast: Cadwal and I
Will play the cook and servant.

GUIDERIUS

I'm tired out.

ARVIRAGUS

Work's made me weak, but strong in appetite. 5

GUIDERIUS

There is cold meat in the cave, we'll gnaw on that,
While what we've killed is cooked.

BELARIUS (*looking into the cave*)

Wait, don't come in:
It's eating our provisions, or I'd think
A fairy'd landed.   10

GUIDERIUS

What's the matter, sir?

BELARIUS

By Jupiter, an angel! Or, if not,
A god that walks on earth! Behold divineness
No older than a boy!

Imogen enters

IMOGEN

Good fellows, please don't harm me: 15
Before I entered, I called out, and meant
To buy or ask for what I took: I swear,
I've stolen nothing, wouldn't even if I'd found
Gold lying there. Here's money for my meat.

GUIDERIUS

Money, youth?   20

ARVIRAGUS

Let all that's gold and silver turn to dirt
Since those who hoard and worship it are those
Who worship dirty gods.

IMOGEN

I see you're angry:
Know, if you kill me for my deed, I would   25
Have died had I not done it.

BELARIUS

Where are you going?

75

IMOGEN

To Milford-Haven.

BELARUS

What's your name?

IMOGEN

Fidele, sir: a relative of mine   30

Is bound for Italy; he embarked at Milford;

I was going to meet him when, spent with hunger,

I trespassed upon you.

BELARUS

Please, my good youth,

Don't think us rude, nor judge our characters   35

By this rough place we live in. Welcome here!

Boys, bid him welcome.

GUIDERIUS

Were you a woman, youth,

I'd woo you hard, but make you an honest one:

I'd buy what I bid for.   40

ARVIRAGUS

I'll be consoled

That he's a man by loving him as my brother:

Be cheerful, for you've fallen in with friends.

IMOGEN

With friends?

Brothers —   45

(*aside*)

I wish they were, for if they'd been

My father's sons, I'd be a jewel less valued;

My weight and yours, dear Posthumus, would find

More equal balance.

BELARIUS

He's wracked with some distress.   50

76

GUIDERIUS

I'd rid him of it!

ARVIRAGUS

And I, whatever it be.

BELARIUS

Listen, boys.

They whisper together

IMOGEN

Great men,

That had a court no bigger than this cave,   55

Could not surpass these two. Pardon me, gods!

I'd change my sex to be comrades with them,

Since Posthumus is false.

BELARIUS

It shall be so.

It's almost night, you will be warmly fed.   60

Boys, let's prepare our feast. Fair youth, come in;

ARVIRAGUS

You're welcome as night to owls, and morn to larks.

IMOGEN

Thanks, sir.

GUIDERIUS

Now please, come in.

They exit

ACT 3 ◆ SCENE 8

ROME. A PUBLIC PLACE.

Two Senators enter with Tribunes

FIRST SENATOR

This is the substance of Caesar's command:

That since the legions now in Gallia are

Too weak to undertake our wars against

The rebel Britons, we must call upon
The nobles for this undertaking. He   5
Named Caius Lucius governor. To you, the tribunes,
He entrusts this commission: that you will raise
This levy of soldiers. Long live Caesar!

TRIBUNE
Is Lucius general of the forces?

SECOND SENATOR
Yes.   10

TRIBUNE
Remaining now in Gallia?

FIRST SENATOR
With those legions
Which I've mentioned, which your levy of men
Must re-supply: the words of your commission
Will specify the numbers and the time   15
Of their dispatch.

TRIBUNE
We will discharge our duty.

They exit

ACT 4 ◆ SCENE 1

WALES

Cloten enters, alone

CLOTEN

I am near the place where they should be meeting, if Pisanio's
mapped it right. How well his garments fit me! Why shouldn't
his mistress, whose maker was the tailor's maker too, fit me
as well? I mean, the lines of my body are as well-defined as
his; no less young, more strong, not less well-endowed by   5
fortune, far more well-connected, above him in birth, just as
experienced in battle, and more impressive one-on-one —
yet this capricious thing loves him in spite of me. Can you
believe the absurdity? Posthumus, your head (which now is
growing upon your shoulders) will, within an hour, be off,   10
your mistress pillaged, your garments cut to pieces in your
face: and once I'm through with her, I'll boot her back to her
father, who may (perhaps) be a little angry at my roughness:
but my mother, who knows how to control his testiness, will
turn his ire into admiration. My horse is tied up safe — out,   15
sword, and aim for violence! Fortune, help me get my hands
on them.

He exits

ACT 4 ◆ SCENE 2

WALES. IN FRONT OF THE CAVE OF BELARIUS.

Belarius, Guiderius, Arviragus, and Imogen come out of the cave

ARVIRAGUS (*to Imogen*)

Brother, stay here:
Are we not brothers?

IMOGEN

    So man and man should be; 5

    But some clay thinks it's nobler than another

    Despite the dust they share. I am very sick.

GUIDERIUS

    You both go on and hunt, I'll stay with him.

IMOGEN

    Though I am ill, you staying here with me

    Cannot heal me. I am not very sick, 10

    Since I can speak: please, trust me — I'd never rob

    Anyone but myself, and bad thief I'd be,

    For stealing where there's nothing.

GUIDERIUS

    I love you. I've said it —

    As much in weight and in intensity 15

    As I love my dear father.

BELARIUS

    What? How's that?

ARVIRAGUS

    If it be a sin to say so, sir, I include myself

    In my good brother's offense. I don't know why

    I love this youth, and I have heard you say, 20

    Love's reason has no reason. If at the door

    Death pounded, asking who should die, I'd say

    "My father, not this youth."

BELARIUS (*aside*)

    Oh noble blood!

    You show your natural worth! Oh breed of greatness! 25

    They're not my sons, yet love him more than me —

    What miracle is this? Who could he be?

ARVIRAGUS

    Brother, farewell.

IMOGEN

Fair hunting.

ARVIRAGUS

To your health. I'm ready, sir —   30

IMOGEN (*aside*)

These are kind creatures. Gods, what lies I have heard!

Our courtiers say all's savage out of court;

Experience, how you disprove that report!

I am sick still, heart-sick; Pisanio,

I'll swallow your drug now.   35

She drinks the poison

BELARIUS

Please recover,

For you must be our housewife.

IMOGEN

Well, or ill,

I am bound to you.

BELARIUS

And will be always.   40

Imogen goes into the cave

BELARIUS

This youth, distressed as he is, seems to come from

Nobility.

ARVIRAGUS

He sings like an angel!

GUIDERIUS

It's wondrous

How grief and patience, both planted deep in him,   45

Mingle their roots together.

BELARIUS

It is broad daylight. Come, let's go! — Who's there?

Cloten enters

CLOTEN

    I cannot find those runaways — that villain

    Has betrayed me. I feel faint.

BELARIUS

    "Those runaways!"   50

    Does he mean us? I think I know him, he's

    Cloten, the son of the Queen. I fear an ambush.

GUIDERIUS

    There's only one of him: you and my brother

    Go see if others come with him: hurry,

    Leave me alone with him.   55

Belarius and Arviragus exit

CLOTEN

    Wait, what are you

    That flee from me? Some villainous highwaymen?

    I've heard of them. What kind of heel are you?

GUIDERIUS

    I've never heeled like I do now, refraining

    From giving you a heel.   60

CLOTEN

    You are a robber!

    A law-breaker, a villain: surrender, thief.

GUIDERIUS

    To who? To you? What are you?

CLOTEN

    You lowly villain,

    My clothes don't tell you who I am?   65

GUIDERIUS

    No, scoundrel,

    Nor does your tailor either, who made those clothes,

    That seem to be what make you.

ACT 4 ◆ SCENE 2

CLOTEN

Flagrant ruffian,

My tailor did not make them. 70

GUIDERIUS

So get gone,

And thank the man who let them. What a fool —

It's almost wrong to beat you.

CLOTEN

Thuggish scoundrel!

Just hear my name, and tremble. 75

GUIDERIUS

What's your name?

CLOTEN

Cloten, you villain.

GUIDERIUS

Cloten, you double villain could be your name,

And I'd not tremble. Toad, Serpent, or Spider —

Those might alarm me more. 80

CLOTEN

To shock you further,

No, to crush you absolutely, you should know

I am son to the Queen.

GUIDERIUS

Well that's a shame; you seem

Less worthy than your birth. 85

CLOTEN

Aren't you afraid?

GUIDERIUS

Those I respect — the wise — are those I fear;

At fools, I laugh — not fear them.

CLOTEN

Die the death:

When I have slain you with my personal hand,   90
I'll go after those who just ran away:
And on the gates of London stick your heads:
Surrender, savage bandit!

They exit, fighting
Belarius and Arviragus re-enter

BELARIUS

No one came with him?

ARVIRAGUS

Not a single soul: he can't be who you think.   95

BELARIUS

I cannot tell: much time's passed since I saw him,
But that voice, the bursts of speech — they're very Cloten.
Even halfway to manhood, he was blind
To frightening threats: for lacking common sense,
One often can lack fear.   100

ARVIRAGUS

But look, my brother.

Guiderius enters, carrying Cloten's head

GUIDERIUS

This Cloten was a fool, even Hercules
Could not have knocked his brains out, for he had none:
But if I hadn't, my head would be in's arms,
As his is now in mine.   105

BELARIUS

What have you done?

GUIDERIUS

I'm certain I cut off one Cloten's head.
Son to the Queen (or so he called himself)
Who called me traitor, vile bandit, and swore
That by his own hand he would capture us   110
Remove our heads from where (thank gods!) they grow,

And set them on London's gates.

BELARIUS

We're all undone.

GUIDERIUS

Why, worthy father, what do we have to lose

Beyond what he swore to take — our lives? What others   115

Did you find here nearby?

BELARIUS

No single soul

That we could spot: but we must safely assume

He brought attendants. It's improbable

That he would come alone, or that the court   120

Would so permit him: then my fear's not baseless,

If I'm afraid this body has a tail

More perilous than its head.

GUIDERIUS

With his own sword,

Which he brandished against my throat, I took   125

His head from him: I'll throw it in the creek

Behind our rock, so it can swim to sea

And tell the fishes he's the Queen's son, Cloten,

That's all I care about.

He exits

BELARIUS

I fear revenge: 130

I wish you had not done it, Polydore:

Though valor suits you well.

ARVIRAGUS

I wish I had done it:

So that revenge chased me!

BELARIUS

Well, it's done: 135

We'll hunt no more today. Go now to our cave.
You and Fidele play the cooks.

ARVIRAGUS

Poor sick Fidele!
I'll gladly go to him: to regain his color
I'd draw the blood of a whole town of Clotens   140
And call it charity.

He exits

BELARIUS

Oh you goddess,
Nature divine: how you proclaim yourself
In these two princely boys. They are as gentle
As zephyrs blowing below the violet,   145
Too soft to nod its sweet head; yet as rough,
(Their royal blood churned up) as the harshest wind
That grabs the mountain pine around the neck
And makes it bow to the valley.
Yet still I wonder   150
What Cloten's being here with us portends,
Or what his death will bring us.

Guiderius re-enters

GUIDERIUS

Where's my brother?
I have sent Cloten's clothead down the stream,
For delivery to his mother; his body's hostage   155
For his return.

Solemn music

BELARIUS

Hear, Polydore — it's music
From Euriphile's instrument: but why has Cadwal
Begun to play it now? What could it be?

GUIDERIUS

What can he mean? Since my dear mother died   160

It has not sung again. Is Cadwal mad?

Arviragus enters bearing Imogen, dead, in his arms

BELARIUS

Look, here he comes,

And brings there in his arms the dreadful reason

For our blind scolding!

ARVIRAGUS

The bird is dead   165

That we have made so much of.

GUIDERIUS

Sweetest fair rose!

My brother wears you not even half as well

As when you bore your own bloom.

BELARIUS

Blessed thing,   170

Jove knows the man you might have made: but oh,

You died a most rare boy, of melancholy.

How did you find him?

ARVIRAGUS

Rigid, as you see:

And smiling, as if flies tickling his slumber   175

Had made him laugh.

GUIDERIUS

But he only sleeps:

If he is gone, he'll make his grave a bed.

His tomb haunted only by gentle fairies

And worms will not come near.   180

ARVIRAGUS

With fairest flowers

While summer lasts, and I live here, Fidele,

I'll sweeten your sad grave: you will not lack
The flower that's like your face, nor velvet moss,
To warm your corpse in winter —   185

GUIDERIUS

Enough, be done.
Let's bury him, and not drag out with homage
That which we owe him. To th' grave!

ARVIRAGUS

Where should we lay him?

GUIDERIUS

By good Euriphile, our mother.   190

ARVIRAGUS

Let it be:
And let us, Polydore — though now our voices
Are men's, breaking — sing him into the ground,
As we did our mother: use the same melody.

GUIDERIUS

Cadwal —   195
I cannot sing: I'll weep, and speak it with you;
For notes of sorrow out of tune are worse
Than lying priests and seers.

ARVIRAGUS

We'll speak it then.

BELARIUS

Great grief, I see, cures lesser ones, for Cloten   200
Is quite forgotten. He was a queen's son, boys,
And though he approached us as an enemy
Remember, he paid for it: Our foe was princely,
And though you took his life, being our foe,
Still bury him, as a prince.   205

GUIDERIUS

Please then, bring him here;

Coward's bodies are as good as heroes',
When neither are alive.

ARVIRAGUS

If you'll go fetch him,
We'll say our song meanwhile — brother, begin.   210

Belarius exits

GUIDERIUS (*sings*)

Fear no more the heat of the sun,
Nor the furious winter's rages,
Your worldly tasks are done,
You've gone home and taken your wages.
Golden boys and girls all must,   215
Like chimney-sweepers, come to dust.

ARVIRAGUS (*sings*)

Fear no more the strong man's frown,
You are past the tyrant's stroke,
Care no more for food or gown,
What difference between reed and oak?   220
Kings, scholars, doctors, they must
All follow this and come to dust.

GUIDERIUS (*sings*)

Fear no more the lightning-flash

ARVIRAGUS (*sings*)

Nor the dreaded thunder's boom.

GUIDERIUS (*sings*)

Fear not slander, nor blame's lash.   225

ARVIRAGUS (*sings*)

You are done with joy and doom.

BOTH (*sing*)

All lovers young, all lovers must
Submit like you and come to dust.

Belarius re-enters, with Cloten's body

GUIDERIUS

Our funeral rites are done: come, lay him down.

BELARIUS

Here's a few flowers: lay on their faces.   230

Come on, let's go, to pray upon our knees:

In their first mother, earth, they are contained:

Their pleasures here are past — so is their pain.

Belarius, Guiderius, and Arviragus exit

Imogen awakes

IMOGEN

Yes, sir, to Milford-Haven, which is the way?

I thank you: by that bush? Please, is it far?   235

Good Lord, have mercy: is it six miles more?

I've walked all night: now I must lie down and sleep.

(seeing the body of Cloten)

But wait! A bedfellow! Oh gods and goddesses!

These flowers are like the pleasures of the world;

This bloody man its burden. I hope I dream: 240

For in one dream I thought I lived in a cave,

Cooking for honest men. But it's not so:

It was a bolt of nothing, shot at nothing,

Which the brain makes from fumes. Our very eyes

Are sometimes like our judgments, blind.   245

The dream's still here: even when I wake it is

Without me, as within me: not imagined, felt.

A headless man? The garments of Posthumus?

I know the shape of his leg: this is his hand:

His foot, like Mercury's: his Martial thigh: 250

The brawn of Hercules: but his face, like Jove's —

Murder in heaven! How — ? It's gone. Pisanio,

Conspiring with that irregulous devil, Cloten,

You've here cut down my lord. Damned Pisanio

Has with his cruel forged letters (damned Pisanio!)   255
Struck down the tallest mast of what once was
The world's most splendid vessel. Oh, Posthumus,
Where is your head? Where's that? Ay me! where's that?
Pisanio could have killed you through the heart,
And left your head on. How could you, Pisanio?   260
It's he and Cloten: Oh, it's clear, so clear!
The drug he gave me, which he said was precious
And would help cure me, didn't I just find
Murderous to my senses? That confirms it sure:
This is Pisanio's deed, and Cloten — Oh!   265
Give color to my pale cheek with your blood,
That we the more horrid may seem to those
Who come upon us. Oh my lord! my lord!

She falls upon the body

Lucius, Captains, and a Soothsayer enter

LUCIUS

What news from Rome?

CAPTAIN

The senate has stirred up the inhabitants   270
And gentlemen of Italy, and they come
Under the command of bold Iachimo,
Duke Siena's brother.

LUCIUS

When do you expect them?

CAPTAIN

With the next favorable wind.   275

LUCIUS

This readiness
Bolsters our hopes. Command our present forces
Be mustered: have the captains look to it. Now, soothsayer,
What have you dreamed lately of this war's fate?

SOOTHSAYER

Last night the very gods showed me this vision: 280

I saw Jove's bird, the Roman eagle, flying

From the damp south to this part of the west,

Then vanishing in the sunbeams: which portends

Success to the Roman host.

LUCIUS

Dream like that often,   285

And never false. But wait, whose trunk is here?

Without his top? Who's this — a page?

But dead, or sleeping on him?

CAPTAIN

He's alive, my lord.

LUCIUS

Young one, who is this you make your bloody pillow?   290

Why do you care for this sad wreck? What happened?

What are you?

IMOGEN

I am nothing; or if not,

Being nothing would be better. This was my master,

A very valiant Briton, and so good,   295

Who here by bandits lies foully slain. Oh gods!

No more masters like him exist: I could wander

From east to west, serve loyally, and never

Find another master like him.

LUCIUS

You poor, good youth!   300

Your mourning moves me no less deeply than

Your master's blood. Your name, my friend?

IMOGEN

Fidele, sir.

LUCIUS

You prove to be as loyal as you're called.

Your name fits your faith well, your faith your name.   305

Will you take your chance with me? I cannot promise

To be as fine a master, but be sure

I will love you no less. Go with me.

IMOGEN

I'll follow, sir. But first, if't please the gods,

I'll hide my master from the flies, as deep   310

As these poor pickaxes can dig: I'll weep and sigh,

And then, my service to him done, follow you,

As long as you will have me.

LUCIUS

Ay, good youth;

I'll act more as your father than your master.   315

My friends,

This boy has taught us manly duties: bury this man

As we do soldiers. Cheer up, wipe your eyes:

Sometimes a fall leads to a happier rise.

They exit

ACT 4 ◆ SCENE 3

A ROOM IN CYMBELINE'S PALACE

Cymbeline, Lords, Pisanio, and Attendants enter

CYMBELINE

Go back: and bring me word of her condition.

Attendant exits

She's ill due to the absence of her son;

Madness that puts her life in danger: oh gods,

How deeply you afflict me! Imogen,

Who gave my life great joy, is gone: my queen   5

Lies on her deathbed, and at a time

When fearful wars threaten me: her son gone,
So needed now. It cuts me deep, beyond
All hope of comfort. And as for you,
Who must know how and when she left here, but   10
Feign ignorance, we'll force it out of you
By a sharp torture.

PISANIO

Sir, my life is yours,
I humbly offer it to you: but my mistress,
I know nothing of where she went nor why,   15
Nor when she will return. I beg your Highness,
Have faith that I am loyal.

FIRST LORD

Honored liege,
The day that she was missing, he was here:
I believe he tells the truth. For Lord Cloten,   20
No effort has been spared in seeking him,
And he'll no doubt be found.

CYMBELINE

Crises besiege us.

(to Pisanio)

We'll let you go for now, but our suspicion
Still lingers on.   25

FIRST LORD

If it please your majesty,
The Roman legions have landed on your coast
With a supply of Roman lords, sent by the Senate.

CYMBELINE

Oh for the counsel of my son and queen!
Now let's withdraw   30
And meet the time, as it seeks us. We fear not
What comes from Italy now to vex us, but
Events here grieve us deeply. Let us go!

Cymbeline, Lords, and Attendants exit

PISANIO

I've had no letter from Posthumus since
I wrote that Imogen was slain. It's strange: 35
Nor have I heard from her, who had promised
To send me tidings often. And I know
Nothing of Cloten's fate, but here remain
Perplexed by it all. The heavens must still work.
In any way I'm false, I'm honest; not true, to be true.   40
The King will see I love my country and how
Bravely I fight these wars, or fall in them:
All other doubts, by time let them be cleared:
Fortune brings in some boats that are not steered.

He exits

ACT 4 ◆ SCENE 4

WALES. IN FRONT OF THE CAVE OF BELARIUS.

Belarius, Guiderius, and Arviragus enter

GUIDERIUS

The battle's all around us.

BELARIUS

Let's move away.

ARVIRAGUS

We'll find no pleasure in life by cutting it off
From action and adventure!

GUIDERIUS

He's right, what hope   5
Is there in hiding? If we do, the Romans
Will either assume we're Britons and slay us or
Recruit us to their cause as barbarous rebels
While it serves them, and slay us after.

95

BELARIUS

I'm known   10
By many in the army: and the King
Deserves neither my service nor your love.

GUIDERIUS

To the army, please:
They do not know my brother and me; and you're
So far gone from their minds, your beard so long,   15
They will not question us.

ARVIRAGUS

By this sun that shines
I'll go: how shameful that I never yet
Have seen a man die, have scarcely seen blood
But that of cowardly hares, lewd goats, and venison!   20
Never mounted a horse! I am ashamed
To look upon the holy sun, to have
The benefit of his blessed beams, remaining
So long unseen, unknown.

GUIDERIUS

By heavens, I'll go.   25
If you will bless me, sir, and give me leave,
I'll be better protected: but if you won't,
I'll risk what danger the Romans may inflict
For my disobedience!

ARVIRAGUS

Me too, amen.   30

BELARIUS

Let's go, boys!
If fighting in your country's wars you die,
Then that's my bed too, lads, and there I'll lie.
Lead, lead. (*aside*) It's time, all else their blood will scorn
'Til it can fly and show they are princes born.   35

They exit

ACT 5 ◆ SCENE 1

BRITAIN. THE ROMAN CAMP.

Posthumus enters, alone

POSTHUMUS

    Yes, bloody cloth, I'll keep you: I'm the one

    Who wished you stained like this. You married folk,

    If you did what I've done, how many of you

    Would be murdering wives much better than yourselves

    For straying just a little? O Pisanio,   5

    Good servants aren't bound to all commands:

    Just honorable ones. Oh gods, if you

    Had punished my faults fairly, I'd never have

    Survived to see this through; you should have saved

    The noble Imogen, to redeem herself,   10

    And struck down me — this wretch! — (more worth your

        vengeance).

    But you chose Imogen; bless me with meekness

    To accept your blessed will. I have come here

    Among the Roman gentry, and to fight

    Against my lady's kingdom; it's enough   15

    That, Britain, I have killed your mistress: peace,

    I will not wound you too. Therefore, good heavens,

    Hear my plan patiently. I will remove

    The Italian weeds I wear, and dress myself

    As British peasants do.   20

(he disrobes)

    Just so, I'll fight

    Against whom I've come with: just so, I'll die

    For you, oh Imogen, even while my life

With every breath, brings death like this, unknown,
Unpitied and unhated, to danger's arms   25
I'll dedicate myself, and let men know
There's more valor in me than my clothes show.
Gods, put the strength of the Leonati in me!
To shame the world's false ways, I will begin
A new fashion: less without, and more within.   30

He exits

ACT 5 ◆ SCENE 2

FIELD BETWEEN THE BRITISH AND ROMAN CAMPS

*Lucius, Iachimo, and the Roman army enter at one door and the
British army at another. Leonatus Posthumus follows, like a poor
soldier. They march over and go out. Iachimo and Posthumus enter
again, skirmishing; Posthumus vanquishes Iachimo and disarms
him, then leaves him.*

IACHIMO

The heaviness and guilt within my heart
Uproot my manhood: I've slandered a lady,
The princess of this country, and its very air
Enfeebles me in revenge; how else could this rube,
A crude, wild slave of Nature have subdued me?   5
If your gentry, Britain, can surpass
This brute as he outdoes our lords, chance is
That we scarcely are men, and you are gods.

He exits

*The battle continues: the Britons flee, Cymbeline is taken prisoner.
Then Belarius, Guiderius, and Arviragus enter to rescue him.*

BELARIUS

Stand, stand. We have the advantage on this ground;
The lane is guarded: nothing routs us but   10
The villainy of our fears.

GUIDERIUS AND ARVIRAGUS

Stand, stand, and fight!

Posthumus enters and reinforces the Britons.
They rescue Cymbeline and exit.
Then Lucius re-enters with Iachimo and Imogen.

LUCIUS

Run far, boy, from the troops, and save yourself:
For friends kill friends — so great is the chaos,
War seems to wear a blindfold.   15

They exit

ACT 5 ♦ SCENE 3

ANOTHER PART OF THE BATTLEFIELD

Posthumus and a British Lord enter

LORD

Did you come from where they made the stand?

POSTHUMUS

I did,

Though you, it seems, fled more than stood.

LORD

I did.

POSTHUMUS

No blame lies on you, sir, for all was lost   5
Until the heavens fought: the King himself
Stripped of both wings of troops, the army broken,
And just the backs of Britons visible;
Flying away through a narrow lane; the enemy
On fire, tongues out like tigers on the hunt,   10

LORD

Where was this lane?

POSTHUMUS

Near the battle, walled in by earth and ditches —

99

Which gave the advantage to an ancient soldier,
(An honest one, I'd swear) who showed he's worth
A lineage as lengthy as his beard,   15
By doing this for his country. Straddling the lane,
He, with two youths (lads more likely to play
A battle game than to commit such slaughter),
Obstructed the passage, crying to those that fled,
"In Britain deer die fleeing, not our men: 20
Stand! face the enemy: stand, stand!" These three,
Three thousand in courage — in action, more —
For three who act are the whole army when
The rest do nothing — with this word, "Stand! stand!"
Having gained the better ground, enchanted more   25
With their own nobleness, revived their spirits;
And those who'd turned cowards became like them,
Grinning as fierce as lions! Then the pursuers
Halted; retreated; then a sudden flight,
A rout, destruction quick: suddenly they fly,   30
Chickens where they'd swooped as eagles: slaves,
Retracing where they strutted victors: and our cowards,
Like crumbs in times of hardship now became
What gave us life; now seeing Roman backs
And exposed hearts, oh heavens, how they wound!   35

LORD

What strange luck!
A narrow lane, an old man, and two boys.

POSTHUMUS

Don't wonder at it: Will you write a rhyme,
Reciting it for laughs? Here's one for you:
Two boys, an old man twice a boy, a lane   40
Saved Britain, and became the Romans' bane.

LORD

Please don't be angry, sir.

POSTHUMUS

Right, to what end?

He who won't face his foe, I'll be his friend:

For if he'll do as he was made to do,   45

I know he'll quickly flee my friendship too.

You've put me into rhyme.

LORD

Farewell, you're angry.

He exits

POSTHUMUS

Still running! This is a lord! Oh noble wretch,

Today how many would have given their lordships   50

To have saved their carcasses? They took flight

To do it, and died anyway. But I,

Whose sorrow seems to be a lucky charm,

Could not find Death even where I heard him roar,

Nor feel him where he struck. Well I'll find you, Death: 55

Though I just sided with the Britons, now I'll look

British no more. I will take up again

The role I played when I came. I'll fight no more,

But give myself up to the lowliest peon

That tries to arrest me. My sentence is death: 60

On either side I come to spend my breath;

I won't protect nor leave with it again,

But end it by some means for Imogen.

Two British Captains enter, with Soldiers

FIRST CAPTAIN

Great Jupiter be praised, Lucius is captured:

The old man and his sons are being called angels.   65

SECOND CAPTAIN

There was a fourth man, dressed in peasant garb,
Who launched the attack with them.

FIRST CAPTAIN

That's the report:
But none of 'em can be found. Stop! who's there?

POSTHUMUS

A Roman, 70
Who would not be so weak now if his seconds
Had shown such valor as he.

SECOND CAPTAIN

Grab him: no dog,
No puniest limb of Rome will return to tell
Stories of the crows that pecked him here: he brags 75
As if he held some rank: take him to the King.

> *Cymbeline, Belarius, Guiderius, Arviragus,*
> *Pisanio, and Roman Captives enter.*
> *The Captains present Posthumus to Cymbeline,*
> *who hands him off to a Jailor.*
> *They exit.*

ACT 5 ◆ SCENE 4

BRITAIN. AN OPEN PLACE NEAR THE BRITISH CAMP.

FIRST JAILOR

No one can help you flee, you're bound by chains:
So graze, if you can find grass.

SECOND JAILOR

Or the stomach.

> *The Jailors exit*

POSTHUMUS

Welcome then, Bondage; for you are the path,
I think, to liberty: I'm sorry — is that enough? 5

Children try to appease mortal fathers that way;
Gods are more full of mercy. If I'm to repent,
The best way I can do it is in chains.
Gods, ask no more sacrifice from me than life:
I know you're more forgiving than vile men,   10
Who from their ruined debtors take a third,
A sixth, a tenth, so they gamble again
On what's left of measly dregs: I don't want that.
For Imogen's dear life take mine, and though
It is worth less, it's still a life; you coined me —   15
Though my own coins are counterfeit, take them.
Oh Imogen! I'll speak to you in silence.

He sleeps. Solemn music.

The ghost of Sicilius Leonatus, father to Posthumus, appears as
an old man dressed as a warrior. He leads by the hand an ancient
matron (his wife, and mother to Posthumus), as music plays.
Then, following other music, the ghosts of the two brothers of
Posthumus enter, bearing the wounds that killed them in the wars.
The ghosts circle around Posthumus as he lies sleeping.

SICILIUS

No more, Jupiter thunder-master,
spite we mortal flies!

MOTHER

My poor son's done nothing but good,   20
whose face we never saw.

SICILIUS

I died while in the womb he stayed
awaiting nature's law.

MOTHER

His father then (for to orphans
you are father, they claim)   25
You should have been, and shielded him

from this earth-shattering pain.

FIRST BROTHER

Why did you let him marry, Jove,
to then be exiled, thrown
Far from his birthplace, cast away
from her his dearest one,
Sweet Imogen?

SECOND BROTHER

Why did you allow Iachimo,
slight thing of Italy,
To taint his nobler heart and brain
with needless jealousy?

MOTHER

Jupiter, since our son is good,
lift off his misery.

SICILIUS

Peek through your tall cloud mansion, help,
or we poor ghosts will cry
To th'other gods and beg their help
against your judgment high.

BROTHERS

Help, Jupiter, or we appeal,
and from your justice fly.

Jupiter descends among thunder and lightning, sitting on an eagle.
He throws a thunderbolt. The Ghosts fall to their knees.

JUPITER

Enough! You petty spirits from down so low
Offend our hearing: hush! How dare you ghosts
Accuse the thunderer, whose bolt you know
From heaven batters all rebelling coasts?
Those I love best, I thwart; so that my gift,

Delayed, deepens delight. Now be content: 50
Your son, laid low, we godly will uplift,
Comfort comes soon, his trial almost spent:
He was born under Jupiter, and in
Our temple he was married. Rise, you shades,
He shall be lord of lady Imogen,   55
And by his suffering he'll be happier made.
Lay this divine book on his breast; inside
We've written his full fortune in these lines
And so, be gone: no more will I abide.
Contain your impatience, or you'll stir up mine.   60
Rise, eagle, to Olympus we will ride.

Jupiter ascends to the heavens.
The Ghosts lay the divine book on Posthumus, and vanish.
Posthumus begins to wake.

POSTHUMUS

Sleep, you've made me your grandson by begetting
A father for me: and you have created
A mother and two brothers: oh, cruel joke!
Gone! Disappeared as soon as they were born: 65
And now I am awake. Poor wretches, who depend
On favors from those greater, dream as I have,
Wake, and find nothing. No, I am mistaken:
Some never dream of longings, nor deserve them,
Yet are dripping in blessings; so am I,   70
Given this lustrous gift, knowing not why.
What fairies haunt this ground? A book? Oh treasure,
Don't be, like our false-glittering world, a garment
Nobler than what it covers. Let what's inside
Be like th'outside, unlike our courtiers, and   75
As good as what you promise.

(*he reads*)

    "When a lion's cub, lost to himself, shall without seeking find,
    and be embraced by, a piece of tender air; and when from a
    stately cedar, branches are cut off, and, after lying dead for
    many years, revive again, rejoin the old trunk, and grow anew,   80
    then shall Posthumus' miseries come to an end, and Britain
    find good fortune and flourish in peace and plenty."
    It's still a dream, or nonsense that madmen
    Spew mindless from their tongues: or both, or nothing,
    Or senseless speaking, or a speech that sense   85
    Cannot unravel. Be it what it is,
    The tangle of my life resembles it;
    I'll keep it, if only to commiserate.

                    The Jailors re-enter

FIRST JAILOR

    Come, sir, are you ready for death?

POSTHUMUS

    Over-roasted, really: ready long ago.   90

FIRST JAILOR

    The word is you'll be strung up, sir; if you're ready for that,
    you're well cooked.

POSTHUMUS

    So, if I prove to be a fine feast for the spectators, the dish will
    be worth the bill.

FIRST JAILOR

    An expensive one for you, sir: but the comfort is that you will   95
    no longer be chased down for payments, fear no more tav-
    ern-bills which buy you as much sorrow when you leave as
    they did mirth: you come in fainting for lack of meat, depart
    reeling with too much drink: sorry that you paid too much,
    and sorry that you'll keep paying for it. Oh, the charity of   100

a hangman's rope! It liquidates thousands in a wink, and in
that way discharges the debt.

POSTHUMUS

I'm happier to die than you are to live.

FIRST JAILOR

Indeed, sir, a sleeping man does not feel a toothache: but look
here, sir: you don't know which way you'll be going.   105

POSTHUMUS

Yes, indeed I do, fellow.

FIRST JAILOR

So you think your dead skull will have eyes in its head? I've
never seen death pictured like that, Well, whichever direc-
tion you head in when your journey ends is something I
don't think you'll be coming back to tell us.   110

A Messenger enters

MESSENGER

Knock off his manacles — bring your prisoner to the King.

POSTHUMUS

You bring good news — Death calls me to liberation.

FIRST JAILOR

I'll be hanged then.

POSTHUMUS

You would then be freer than a jailor: no shackles for the dead.

All exit except the First Jailor

FIRST JAILOR

I never saw one so eager, unless there was a man who wished 115
to marry a gallows, and beget young nooses. Even rogues
worse than him die against their will — as I would, were I
one. Oh, I wish there were no jailors or gallowses! I may not
profit off what I'm saying, but I'd be better off for it.

They exit

ACT 5 ◆ SCENE 5

CYMBELINE'S TENT

Cymbeline, Belarius, Guiderius, Arviragus, Pisanio, Lords,
Officers, and Attendants enter

CYMBELINE

Stand by my side, you whom the gods have made

Preservers of my throne: my heart regrets

That the poor soldier that so nobly fought,

Whose rags shamed gilded arms, cannot be found.

BELARIUS

I never saw   5

Such noble fury in so poor a thing.

CYMBELINE

No news of him?

PISANIO

They've searched for him among the dead and living;

But there's no trace.

CYMBELINE

To my grief, I have inherited   10

The reward that should be his,

(*to Belarius, Guiderius, and Arviragus*)

to which I'll add

You three: the liver, heart, and brain of Britain.

By those — your passion, affection and reason —

She has survived. And now it's time   15

To ask from where you came. Declare yourselves.

BELARIUS

Sir,

In Wales here we were born, as gentlemen:

To boast further would not be true nor modest,

Unless I add we are honest.   20

CYMBELINE

Bow your knees:

Arise my knights o'th'battle.

(*Cornelius and Ladies enter, with sad faces*)

Why greet our victory sadly?

CORNELIUS

Oh hail, great King!

To sour your happiness, I must report   25

The Queen is dead.

CYMBELINE

How did she die?

CORNELIUS

In horror, madly dying. If you'll allow me,

I'll share what she confessed.

CYMBELINE

Please speak.   30

CORNELIUS

First, she confess'd she never loved you, only

Married your royalty, was wife to your rank:

Abhorred your person.

CYMBELINE

She never told me this:

And were they not her dying words, I'd not   35

Believe her lips would let them pass. Proceed.

CORNELIUS

Your daughter, whom she always claimed to love

With such integrity, she then confessed

Stung her sight like a scorpion, whose life

(Had her escape not foiled it) she had planned   40

To end with poison.

CYMBELINE

O you artful fiend!

Can anyone read a woman? Is there more?

CORNELIUS

More, sir, and worse. She did confess she had

For you a fatal venom, which, when taken,   45

Would suck the life from you minute by minute,

Consuming you by inches. Meanwhile, she planned —

By weeping, nursing, tending to you, kissing —

To convince you through her masquerade to adopt

Her son as heir; but failing, by his absence,   50

Grew shameless-desperate; she divulged her plans

(Defying heaven and men), regretted that

The evils she hatched were not accomplished, and

Despairing, died.

CYMBELINE

Did you, her women, hear this?   55

LADY

We did, so please your Highness.

CYMBELINE

My eyes

Were not at fault, for she was beautiful:

Nor my ears that heard her flattery, nor my heart

That thought her what she seemed. To have questioned it   60

Would not have been noble: yet, O my daughter,

You may say it was folly in me not to do so,

And your experience may prove it. Heaven mend us!

Lucius,Iachimo, the Soothsayer, and other Roman prisoners enter,

guarded; behind them, Posthumus and Imogen

CYMBELINE

Now, Caius Lucius, it's not for taxes you come;

The Britons have scratched out that pledge, though it cost   65

Many brave lives. Their souls may be appeased

With slaughtering you, our captives, which we've granted.

LUCIUS

    Remember, sir, luck wins a war: the day
    Was yours by accident — had it gone to us,
    We would not, when our blood was cool, have threatened   70
    Our prisoners with the sword. One thing I entreat:
    That you will let my boy (a Briton born) —
    Be ransomed: never has a master had
    A page so kind, so diligent, devoted,
    So tender; he has done no Briton harm,   75
    Although he's served a Roman. Save him, sir,
    If that's the only blood you spare.

CYMBELINE

    I know I've seen him:
    His face is so familiar to me. Boy,
    Your looks have carried you into my grace,   80
    And you are mine. I don't know why, for what reason
    To say, "live, boy": don't thank your master, live;
    And ask of Cymbeline what favor you wish,
    I'll give it to you.

IMOGEN

    I humbly thank your Highness.   85

LUCIUS

    I did not ask for you to plead my life, good lad,
    And yet I know you will.

IMOGEN

    No, no — I'm sorry,
    There's something else I must do: I see a thing
    Bitter to me as death.   90

LUCIUS

    The boy disdains me.
    Why is he so distressed?

                 Imogen stares at Iachimo

CYMBELINE

What is it, boy?

I love you more and more. Do you know this man?

Speak, should he live? Is he your kin? Your friend? 95

IMOGEN

He is a Roman, no more kin to me

Than I to your Highness.

CYMBELINE

Why do you stare at him so?

IMOGEN

I'll tell you, sir, in private, if you please

To hear me out. 100

CYMBELINE

Ay, ay, with all my heart,

And with my best attention. What's your name?

IMOGEN

Fidele, sir.

CYMBELINE

You're my good youth: my page

I'll be your master: walk with me: speak freely. 105

Cymbeline and Imogen walk side by side

BELARIUS

Has this boy come back from death?

ARVIRAGUS

Two grains of sand

Could not be more alike than he and Fidele!

What do you think?

GUIDERIUS

That what was dead's alive. 110

BELARIUS

Creatures may be alike: if it's he, I'm sure

He would have spoken to us.

PISANIO (*aside*)

    It is my mistress:

    Since she is living, let our fates run on,

    Towards good or bad.   115

           Cymbeline and Imogen come forward

CYMBELINE (*to Iachimo*)

    Sir, step forward,

    Answer this boy's demands, and honestly,

    Or, by our greatness, bitter torture will

    Winnow the truth from falsehood. Go on, speak to him.

IMOGEN

    My request is for this gentleman to say   120

    From whom he got that ring.

POSTHUMUS (*aside*)

    What's that to him?

IACHIMO

    I am glad to be compelled to utter that

    Which torments me to conceal. By villainy

    I got this ring: it's Posthumus' jewel —   125

    He whom you banished. Should I say more, my lord?

CYMBELINE

    All that's part of this.

IACHIMO

    That paragon, your daughter,

    For whom my heart bleeds — forgive me, please — I faint.

CYMBELINE

    My daughter? What about her? Rouse your strength: 130

    I'd rather you stay alive while Nature lets you

    Than die before I hear more: try, man, speak!

IACHIMO

    Once 'pon a time, unhappy was the clock

    That struck the hour: it was in Rome — I curse

The mansion where — 'twas at a feast — Oh I wish   135
Our food had been poisoned (or at least
That which I swallowed) — the good Posthumus
(What should I say? He was too good to be
Where vile men were) was sitting sadly there,
Hearing us praise our loves from Italy   140
For beauty that made barren the swollen boast
Of our best speaker —

CYMBELINE
I'm going to explode.
Come to the point.

IACHIMO
Sir, all too soon I will,   145
But you may want grief fast and suddenly.
Posthumus, noble lord ,then took his turn,
And he (while not unpraising those we praised —
'Bout this he was very polite) began
To paint his mistress' picture with his words —   150

CYMBELINE
Come on, to the point!

IACHIMO
Your daughter's chastity (here it begins) —
He spoke as if even virgin Diana
Had too-hot dreams, and only she stayed cool:
Then I, the wretch, disputed him, and wagered   155
Pieces of gold 'gainst this (which he then wore
Upon his honored finger) to attain,
By wooing, his place in bed, and win this ring
By her and my adultery. Then to Britain
I fly, a plan in mind; and you may, sir,   160
Remember me at court, where I was taught
By your chaste daughter the vast difference

'Tween amorous and villainous. Being dampened
In hope, not longing, my Italian brain
(In this your duller Britain) started scheming   165
Most vilely: but advancing my own aims.
And to be brief, my trickery so prevailed,
That I returned with proof deceitful enough
To drive the noble Leonatus mad,
By wounding his faith in her reputation,   170
With this her bracelet (oh cunning, how I got it!)
And providing details of secret marks
Upon her body, so he could not help
But think her bond of chastity quite cracked,
And then — I think I see him now —   175

POSTHUMUS (*revealing himself*)

You do,
Italian fiend! I am a fool, a murderer,
The worst who lived — Some righteous avenger, give
Me rope, a knife, poison! King, send for torturers,
Your most inventive ones: for it is I   180
Who elevate the most abhorred things on earth
By being worse than they. I am Posthumus,
That killed your daughter — but villain-like, I lie:
That forced a lesser villain than myself,
A sacrilegious thief, to do it. The temple   185
Of virtue was she; no, virtue itself.
Spit, and throw stones, cast filth upon me. Oh Imogen!
My queen, my life, my wife — Oh Imogen,
Imogen, Imogen!

IMOGEN

Peace, my lord, hear, hear —   190

POSTHUMUS

You think this is a farce? Mocking page,

Your role lies there.

Striking her, she falls

PISANIO

Oh, my lord Posthumus!

You never killed Imogen till now. Help, help!

My honored lady!   195

CYMBELINE

Has the world turned upside down?

POSTHUMUS

What's this? The ground collapses —

PISANIO

Wake, my mistress!

CYMBELINE

If this be her, the gods intend to strike me

To death with mortal joy.   200

PISANIO

How is my mistress?

IMOGEN

Oh get away from me!

You gave me poison — wicked scoundrel, go!

Don't even breathe near princes.

CYMBELINE

Imogen's tune!   205

PISANIO

May gods strike me with thunderbolts if I

Am lying: I thought the box I gave you was

A precious thing: I got it from the Queen.

CYMBELINE

There's more still?

IMOGEN

But it poison'd me.   210

CORNELIUS

Oh gods!

I left out one thing which the Queen confessed,

Which will then prove you honest. "If Pisanio,"

She said, "has given his mistress that potion

Which I told him was medicine, she's been treated   215

As I would treat a rat."

CYMBELINE

What's this, Cornelius?

CORNELIUS

The Queen, sir, very often pressured me

To concoct poisons for her, with the excuse

Of practicing her knowledge on vile creatures.   220

Suspecting her intentions, I made instead

A substance which when taken would arrest

The present power of life, but in short time

Would restore all natural functions. Have you tried it?

IMOGEN

Most likely I did, for I was dead.   225

BELARIUS

My boys,

There was our error.

GUIDERIUS

This is our Fidele!

IMOGEN

Why did you cast your wedded lady from you?

Believe now you stand on a rock, and cast   230

For me again.

She embraces him

POSTHUMUS

Hang here like fruit, my soul,

'Til this tree die.

117

CYMBELINE
What's this, my flesh, my child?
Will you not speak to me?   235
IMOGEN (*kneeling*)
Your blessing, sir.
BELARIUS (*to Guiderius and Arviragus*)
I cannot blame you for loving this youth.
You had a motive for it.
CYMBELINE
May my tears
Fall on you like holy water. Imogen,   240
The Queen is dead.
IMOGEN
I am sorry for it, my lord.
CYMBELINE
Oh, she was wicked; it's because of her
That we meet here as strangers: but her son
Is gone, we know not how, nor where.   245
PISANIO
My lord,
Now my fear's gone, I'll speak the truth. Lord Cloten,
When my lady went missing, came to me
Swearing if I did not reveal where she was,
He'd kill me instantly. By accident,   250
I carried a feigned letter from my master —
'Twas in my pocket — which led Cloten to
Go seek her on the mountains next to Milford;
Where in a frenzy, in my master's garments,
(Which he had forced from me) away he rushed   255
With an impure intent, swearing he'd violate
My lady's honor; what became of him
After that, I don't know.

GUIDERIUS

    Let me end the story:

    I slew him there.   260

CYMBELINE

    Gods no, don't let that be!

    I don't want your good deeds to have to force

    A hard sentence from my lips: please, you brave youth,

    Now take it back.

GUIDERIUS

    I've said it, and I did it.   265

CYMBELINE

    He was a prince.

GUIDERIUS

    A most uncivil one. The wrongs he did me

    Were not prince-like; so I cut off his head,

    And am right glad he is not standing here

    To tell this tale of me.   270

CYMBELINE

    I grieve for you:

    By your own tongue you are condemned, and must

    Endure our law: you're dead.

IMOGEN

    That headless man

    I then thought was my lord.   275

CYMBELINE

    Seize the offender,

    Remove him from our presence.

BELARIUS

    Wait, sir King.

    This man is better than the man he slew,

    As well descended as yourself, and has   280

    Merited more from you than an army of Clotens.

CYMBELINE

Why, old soldier:

Will you taste of our wrath? How of descent

As good as ours?

ARVIRAGUS

In that, he went too far.   285

CYMBELINE

And you shall die for it.

BELARIUS

We will die all three,

Unless I prove that two of us are as good

As I have claimed he is. My sons, I must

Let loose words that are dangerous to me,   290

But may benefit you.

ARVIRAGUS

Your danger's ours.

GUIDERIUS

And our good his.

BELARIUS

I'll speak, if you'll allow:

You had, great King, a subject, who   295

Was called Belarius. —

CYMBELINE

What of him? He is

A banished traitor.

BELARIUS

Indeed a banished man,

A traitor, I don't know how.   300

CYMBELINE

Take him away,

The whole world will not save him.

BELARIUS

Not too fast;

First pay me for the nursing of your sons,

CYMBELINE

Nursing of my sons?   305

BELARIUS

I am too blunt and brazen: here's my knee:

Before I rise I will champion my sons;

Then spare not their old father. Mighty sir,

These two young gentlemen that call me father

And think they are my sons, are none of mine;   310

They are the issue of your loins, my liege,

And blood of your begetting.

CYMBELINE

How? my issue?

BELARIUS

Sure as you are your father's. I (old Morgan)

Am that Belarius, whom you once banished: 315

My non-offense, my punishment, and all

My treason were to serve you. (To suffer

Was all the harm I did.) These gentle princes

(For such and so they are) these twenty years

I've raised and taught. Their nurse, Euriphile,   320

(Whom for the theft I wedded) stole these children

Upon my banishment: I persuaded her to.

Beaten for loyalty,

I was driven to treason. Their dear loss,

The more it wounded you, the more it fit   325

My aim in stealing them. But gracious sir,

Here are your sons again, and I must lose

Two of the sweetest companions in the world.

CYMBELINE

You weep, and speak;
The service that you three have done is more   330
Wondrous than this you tell me. I lost my children:
If these be they, I know not how to wish
A pair of worthier sons.

BELARIUS

If you'll allow me;
This gentleman, whom I call Polydore,   335
Most worthy Prince, as yours, was named Guiderius:
This gentleman, my Cadwal, Arviragus,
Your younger princely son; he, sir, was wrapped
In a peculiar mantle, made by hand
By his queen mother, which for further proof   340
I can with ease produce.

CYMBELINE

Guiderius had
Upon his neck a mole, a blood-toned star;
It was a mark of wonder.

BELARIUS

This is he,   345
Who has upon him still that natural stamp:
Nature was wise, bestowing it then,
To be his evidence now.

CYMBELINE

Oh, what am I?
A mother to the birth of three? No mother   350
Ever rejoiced delivery more. Oh Imogen,
You've lost by this a kingdom.

IMOGEN

No, my lord;
I've gained two worlds by it. Oh my gentle brothers,

Have we met then? Oh, from now on never say   355
That I do not speak truth. You called me brother,
When I was but your sister: I, you, "brothers,"
When you were truly so.

CYMBELINE

You've met before?

ARVIRAGUS

Yes, my good lord.   360

GUIDERIUS

And when we met we loved,
Kept loving so, until we thought he died.

CORNELIUS

By the Queen's drug she swallowed.

CYMBELINE

Oh rare instinct!
When shall I hear it all? Where? How'd you live?   365
And when'd you come to serve our Roman captive?
Why did you flee from court? And where to? These
Need to be asked, and more I do not know.
But this time and place
Is not for long interrogations. Look: 370
Posthumus found his anchor, Imogen;
And she (like harmless lightning) throws her eye
On him, her brothers, me, and her Roman, hitting
Each object with her joy: and each return
That joy and more to her. Let's leave this place,   375
And smoke the temple with our ritual thanks.

(*to Belarius*)

You are my brother; we'll hold you so forever.

IMOGEN (*to Belarius*)

You are my father too, and did rescue me,
To see this joyful day.

CYMBELINE

    All overjoyed   380

    Except those still bound: let them be joyful too,

    For they shall taste our comfort.

IMOGEN (*to Lucius*)

    My good master,

    I will yet do you service.

LUCIUS

    Bless you then!   385

CYMBELINE

    That forlorn soldier, that so nobly fought —

    His presence here would have been right, and graced

    The thankings of a king.

POSTHUMUS

    I am, sir,

    The soldier that accompanied these three,   390

    Dressed in poor rags: that I was he,

    Iachimo, tell: I had you down, and might

    Have made an end of you.

IACHIMO (*kneels*)

    I'm down again:

    My conscience sinks me: take that life, I beg you,   395

    Which I owe a thousand times: but your ring first,

    And here, the bracelet of the truest princess

    That ever swore fidelity.

POSTHUMUS

    Kneel not to me:

    The power that I have over you is to spare you: 400

    The malice towards you, to forgive you. Live,

    And deal with others better.

CYMBELINE

    Nobly judged!

We'll learn benevolence from a son-in-law:

Pardon's the word to all.   405

ARVIRAGUS

You helped us, sir,

As if you really meant to be our brother.

We rejoice that you are.

POSTHUMUS

Your servant, Princes. Please, my lord of Rome,

Call forth your soothsayer: as I slept, I thought   410

Great Jupiter, upon his eagle's back,

Appeared to me, with other ghostly illusions

Of my own kin. When I awoke I found

This book upon my chest, whose content

Is so hard and far from sense, that I cannot   415

Glean anything from it. Let him show his

Skill at interpretation.

LUCIUS

Philharmonus!

SOOTHSAYER

Here, my good lord.

LUCIUS

Read, and declare the meaning.   420

SOOTHSAYER (*reads*)

"When a lion's cub, lost to himself, shall without seeking find,
and be embraced by, a piece of tender air; and when from a
stately cedar, branches are cut off, and, after lying dead for
many years, revive again, rejoin the old trunk, and grow anew,
then shall Posthumus' miseries come to an end, and Britain 425
find good fortune and flourish in peace and plenty."

You, Leonatus, are the lion's cub:

The fitting and apt origin of your name,

Being Leo-natus, Lion-born, means much:

125

(*to Cymbeline*)
    The piece of tender air, your virtuous daughter,   430
    Which we call "mollis aer"; and "mollis aer"
    We term mulier, "woman," which I divine
    Is your most constant wife; (*to Posthumus*) even now,
    Fulfilling to the letter the oracle —
    Unknown to you, unsought — you were embraced   435
    By this most tender air.

CYMBELINE
    This makes some sense.

SOOTHSAYER
    The lofty cedar, royal Cymbeline,
    Stands here for you: your lopped branches signify
    Your two lost sons, who by Belarius stolen,   440
    For many years thought dead, are now revived,
    Joined to the majestic cedar, whose progeny
    Promises Britain peace and plenty.

CYMBELINE
    Well,
    My peace we will begin: and, Caius Lucius,   445
    Although the victor, we submit to Caesar,
    And to the Roman empire, promising
    To pay our former tribute, from the which
    We were dissuaded by our wicked queen.

SOOTHSAYER
    The fingers of the powers above do tune   450
    The harmony of this peace. The vision
    Which I explained to Lucius just before
    This scarce-cold battle started, at this instant
    Is fully realized. For the Roman eagle,
    Soaring aloft, wings soaring, south to west   455
    Flew further and further and in the beams of the sun

Vanished; foretelling that our princely eagle,
The imperial Caesar, will again unite
His favor with the radiant Cymbeline,
Who shines here in the west.   460

CYMBELINE

Let's praise the gods,
And let our curling smoke climb to their nostrils
From our blessed altars. We announce this peace
To all our subjects. Let us go; and let
A Roman and a British banner wave   465
As friends together: so through London march,
And in the temple of great Jupiter
We'll ratify our peace: seal it with feasts.
Go on! There never was a war that ceased
('Fore bloody hands were washed) with such a peace.   470

They all exit

END OF PLAY